What are your staff trying to tell you?

WHAT ARE YOUR STAFF TRYING TO TELL YOU?

REVEALING BEST AND WORST PRACTICE IN EMPLOYEE SURVEYS

PETER HUTTON

First published by Lulu.com in 2008.

Revised edition published by Lulu.com in 2009.

ISBN 978-1-4452-4688-8

To Matthew, Edward and Beatrice

Contents

Contents contd.

List of Illustrations

Preface

Whom this book is aimed at

This book has a very specific focus though it is designed to appeal to anyone in any organisation who is involved in undertaking or responding to the findings of an employee survey. This includes those involved in commissioning, or even designing their own, employee surveys. Typically, they would be working in the HR or internal communication functions. It also includes those at a very senior level – CEOs or HR directors – who either delegate the commissioning of an employee survey to others or who take it upon themselves to commission a survey, often without really understanding the potential pitfalls that lie ahead.

There are then a host of managers who may not have been directly involved in commissioning a survey but who, at the end of the process, can be confronted with a batch of survey findings that leave them confused, frustrated or mystified.

Academics and students, particularly those studying organisational and social psychology, should also find this a stimulating read. I hope that it will broaden their understanding of what can be achieved if they consider using a wide range of question techniques in their survey, rather than rely just on the agree/disagree scale, an approach that is the focus of particular attention in this book.

Finally, there are those who are involved in undertaking employee surveys in consultancies or who have a general interest in people management and the measuring tools that go with it.

Why this book was written

Having spent over 30 years in research, written a book and scores of articles on how to use research in management, I increasingly sensed a gap between what clients were looking for and what the research industry was delivering. This was reflected both in my own experiences and in the issues being raised at research conferences and in the industry media. While quantitative (as opposed to qualitative) researchers appeared to have a good reputation for managing process and generating data, they were not necessarily so well regarded for providing insight and relating well to the way their clients' businesses worked.

This was not totally surprising. Research agencies and industry bodies are good at training on the mechanics and processes of proposal writing, questionnaire design, sampling and data analysis, but generally provide little or no training on management theory as it is applied at a senior level in client organisations. Yet this is what provides the frameworks within which the outputs of the research industry are evaluated and interpreted.

As a researcher with a degree in the social sciences, I was particularly interested in the management ideas that lay behind research briefs and the decisions that the research fed in to. The growth of management schools and the management consulting industry over the last forty or so years - particularly in the US - has brought with it a major transformation in the way in which we think about business. This has had significant implications both for management and for the industries that feed it with information, including the (market) research industry.

The 1980s and 1990s were particularly fertile decades for new and radical management ideas. Increasingly, the leading business schools and consultancies wanted to be seen as thought leaders that understood and could map out how business paradigms were changing and the implications this had for achieving corporate success.

Over the long-term, it seems to me that one phenomenon has driven our need constantly to revise our thinking about business and management: the shift in the developed world from economies that were essentially based upon trading and manufacturing *tangible* goods to economies that are now largely based on providing *intangible* services. If you include the public sector, then the vast majority of national income in the developed world is based on the provision of *intangible* services rather than the trading of *tangible* goods.

I believe that three trends in management thinking have had, or should have had, a major impact on research and how it is used in business. These are:

1. A shift from a focus on profit generation to value creation
2. The growth of integrated strategic thinking
3. A growing emphasis on the understanding and measurement of intangible factors in the market and workplace.

In 2006, I presented a paper to the annual ESOMAR Congress in London entitled 'Reconstructing Research for the 21st Century'[1]. In it, I argued that, while leading edge management thinking had moved forward, the market research industry was still largely operating within management paradigms that served business silos that were increasingly being broken down. In some areas, the demand for measurement had gone off on a tangent and created a set of practices that, with hindsight, were not particularly helping the organisations they were meant to be supporting.

What has gone wrong with employee research?

Employee research was one of these. Instead of applying the full range of different question types available to the researcher, much of the industry has defaulted to using just one kind of question – the agree/disagree scale. Moreover, many of the consultancies providing employee research services insist on using their own standard set of agree/disagree statements, irrespective of the nature of their clients and their unique needs.

To me this seemed the antithesis of what research should be about. Surely, what it should be doing is helping businesses understand how their organisations uniquely work and the issues they need to address to achieve their individual objectives and to realise their goals. We should not just be providing generic measures on a standardised scale with the main means of interpretation being how well each organisation scores against the consultancies' norms. Yet this is where, perhaps, 70% of the employee surveys conducted worldwide have ended up.

You might ask, 'So what is wrong with this approach?', and that, briefly, is what this book is about. It also sets out to explore a number of related issues. For example, how is it that the agree/disagree scale has come to dominate the field of employee surveys? How have some consultancies used a variety of statistical techniques to make, perhaps unwittingly, a number of exaggerated and, arguably, erroneous claims about hidden truths that lie within their banks of survey data. Moreover, if the agree/disagree scale is not the survey tool that organisations should be using, then what is?

There are no doubt people who are very wedded to the use of the agree/disagree scale in their employee surveys. They may well dismiss the arguments presented here and point to the many millions of questionnaires that have been completed by employees across the world as proof that they cannot be that bad. That is their prerogative. However, in the social as well as the natural sciences, our understanding deepens through our challenging our assumptions and, where they are found wanting, replacing them with new and more robust assumptions. The assumptions underlying the widespread use of the agree/disagree scale in employee surveys seems to have gone unchallenged for far too long to the detriment of employee research and of people management as a whole.

I hope that people who read this book will end up feeling that what they have read is 'common sense'. In designing questionnaires, the most important thing you can do is to ask yourself your own questions and then be honest about whether or not they really capture what you intend. The second most important thing you can do is to ask yourself whether, when you have asked everyone in an organisation the same questions, you can do anything practical with the results. One of the basic criticisms of many of the surveys that are conducted using the agree/disagree scale is that they fail one, or both, of these simple tests.

To support the arguments of this book, I have used a number of examples. All the examples are taken from real surveys. Many of them are the standardised formulations used regularly by leading consultancies. In some cases, the same questions have been used in hundreds or even thousands of different surveys. I am not of the view that this necessarily makes them good questions, but that is something for you, the reader, to judge after reading the arguments!

Although there is much more to conducting an employee survey than questionnaire design – such as data collection, data analysis and project management – there are plenty of other books that explore these subjects in depth. In this book, I am happy to focus on questionnaire design, and particularly the use and abuse of the agree/disagree scale, and on multivariate analysis where I believe it has compounded some of the problems of over-reliance on that technique.

Structure of the book

The book is divided into four parts. The first explains the role of research among employees and the different kinds of question formulations available to the researcher, including scales.

The second highlights the limitations of the agree/disagree scale technique that has come to dominate the world of employee surveys. It examines the way its use in employee surveys has evolved and how two particular companies - Gallup and Best Companies - have taken its use to an extreme. This section reviews their approaches and asks whether the claims they make for their particular set of idiosyncratic questions stand up to scrutiny. It also questions the validity and usefulness of the agree/disagree scale technique in three areas where it is used extensively:

1. Compiling normative databases
2. Undertaking various kinds of statistical, multivariate analysis on the data and
3. In defining employee engagement

The third part provides a personal view on how best to undertake an employee survey so that it effectively meets the needs and feeds the aspirations of the organisation.

The final part summarises what I believe is wrong with constructing employee surveys that consist (almost) exclusively of agree/disagree scale questions.

Acknowledgements

In preparing this book, I would like to thank four people in particular for their valuable and constructive comments. Andrew Zelin's wise counsel reassured me that what I thought I understood about multivariate analysis was mostly true. Helen Lester's support and thoughtful observations encouraged me to believe that what I was saying was important, even interesting, while making the narrative clearer and flow better. Toni Playell kindly scanned the manuscript for typographical errors and Alan Scott made some valuable observations.

Finally, I would like to thank Ian Dennis of the University of Plymouth whose critique of my understanding of the Likert scale and factor analysis was one of the reasons for my deciding to issue a revised edition of the book.

Peter Hutton, November 2009

PART 1
Employee Surveys and Question Types

PART 1: Employee Surveys and Question Types

Employee surveys in management

Employee surveys can be a powerful management tool. They can test the temperature of the business and identify the things that are motivating staff or driving the business forward. They can tell you how well your systems and processes are working and define the issues you need to address to make them work better. Alternatively, they can produce a great deal of data and fail to provide anything of any value to managing the organisation at all. The key to avoiding the latter is good questionnaire design.

Good questions reveal what is going on. Bad questions obscure it. Good questions point to solutions, bad questions do not. Good questions resonate with staff. Bad questions bemuse them.

Good questions reveal what is going on. Bad questions obscure it. Good questions point to solutions, bad questions do not. Good questions resonate with staff. Bad questions bemuse them

Understanding what your employees believe about the organisation they work in - their aspirations and frustrations, the things that excite them or wear them down - is what managing people is all about. Employee surveys are not the only way of doing this. Indeed, such is the amount of time and effort invested in the planning and execution of an employee survey that they are necessarily undertaken relatively infrequently in most organisations. Therefore, and quite rightly, managers need to rely on their normal day-to-day channels of communication to gauge the mood of their staff and judge their level of understanding of what is going on and what is expected of them. So when an employee survey is undertaken, it needs to provide something extra, something that provides more insight than can be gleaned by any other means and something that will undoubtedly move the organisation forward.

Questionnaire design is one of the principle skills of a researcher. It is a skill that they have to develop over time through lots of practice and heaps of criticism. When an employee survey is undertaken, particular attention needs to be paid to the questions asked – the topics and the exact wording that is used. You only have one crack at this in each survey. If any of the questions are ambiguous, or otherwise poorly worded, it wastes the time of every employee who has willingly given up their time to answer the questionnaire and produces no information that will be of any use to management.

Partly because designing questionnaires that match the unique needs of an organisation is so challenging, many consultancies have simply not bothered. Instead, they have defaulted to a standard set of questions in one particular format. Much of this book is about challenging that approach, drawing attention to the issues it raises and suggesting how to do it better.

In this section, I have set out to explore the different types of questions that are widely used in the (market) research industry, particularly by researchers engaged in undertaking employee surveys.

The range of question types

Anyone who works in an organisation knows what it is like to work there, from their point of view. They also pick up snippets of information from a wide variety of sources that help them build up a picture of what it is like for others working there, where the management is trying to take the business, how successful the organisation is, what is expected of them, how well they are perceived to be doing and so on.

However, everyone has a different experience and a different perspective. Surveys are a way of enabling management and, indeed, staff as a whole, to understand what employees across the organisation think and feel about a very wide range of issues. In this way, management can make more informed and, therefore, better decisions that are in the best interests of both employees and the organisation as a whole.

There are a host of reasons why organisations decide to undertake an employee survey. Perhaps the most common reason might be described as an overall 'body scan' – a survey designed to look at multiple aspects of the organisation to understand what is working well, what is working badly and the issues that need to be addressed to move the organisation forward. Others surveys may be designed to explore a particular aspect of the organisation – internal communications, response to major change programmes, internal branding, remuneration and reward policies and so on.

Surveys can measure many different things, but they can generally be used to explore the following aspects of employees and their work experience:

What they know: Their knowledge

What they believe: Their beliefs

What they feel: Expressed by their attitudes

What they think: Their opinions

What they do: Their behaviours

Why they do what they do: Their motivations

Who they are: Their objective characteristics e.g. gender, age, department, length of service

All these are relevant to understanding how an organisation works and identifying the issues that will make it work better.

The art of questionnaire design is about constructing exactly the right questions to provide management with the information it needs on any particular topic to enable it to make better decisions.

On the face of it, undertaking a survey sounds very simple; all you need to do is to list out some questions, send them out to people, get them to answer and send them back then tally all the results. The reality, though, is considerably more challenging. Designing questions that are unambiguous, that provide actionable information and that do not raise more questions than they answer, is a skill that, in my experience, has to be learnt over many years and through actually doing it. It is an art that you can never stop learning.

Some questions, it is true, can be standardised. Once they have been seen to provide useful information in one organisation then they can often be used in other organisations. Rating overall job satisfaction is probably the most common example. However, every organisation is unique and will have its own issues that need to be approached in a bespoke way. This is where the skill of a researcher comes in to play.

There are literally thousands of different questions that can be asked in an employee survey. However, they actually reduce to just three types: They are either:

> **Scale questions** – from a simple 'yes' or 'no' through to three-, four-, five- or even ten-point numerical or verbal scales.
>
> OR
>
> **List questions** – employees are asked to select items from a list of items that meet a specified criterion.
>
> OR
>
> **Open-ended questions** – respondents are asked to say, in their own words, what they think or feel about a particular topic or issue.

However, within these categories there are scores of different types of scales, lists and open-ended questions that can be asked about different facets of the organisation and what employees feel/experience whilst working in it.

Below I have listed some of the more commonly used types of questions, along with some more unusual formulations that I have developed over the years. In developing questions, it is worth thinking very carefully about what type of information would really enable you to understand best the issues the organisation is facing.

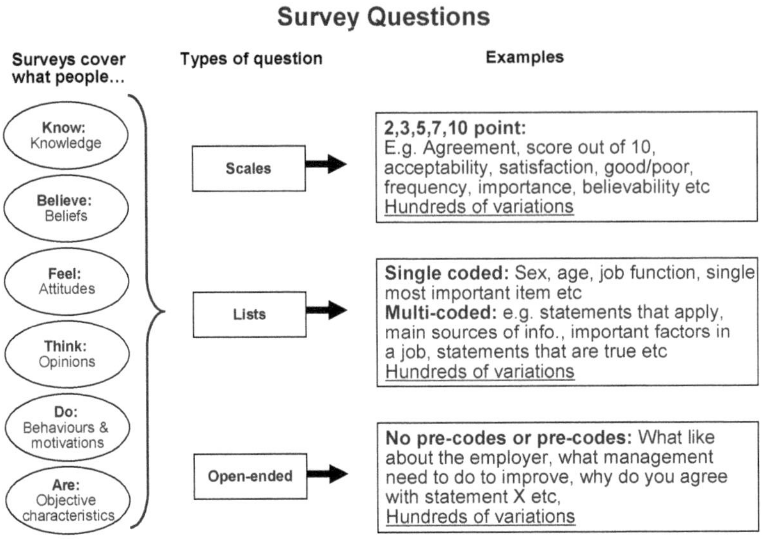

Survey Questions

Surveys cover what people...	Types of question	Examples
Know: Knowledge; Believe: Beliefs	Scales	**2,3,5,7,10 point:** E.g. Agreement, score out of 10, acceptability, satisfaction, good/poor, frequency, importance, believability etc <u>Hundreds of variations</u>
Feel: Attitudes; Think: Opinions	Lists	**Single coded:** Sex, age, job function, single most important item etc **Multi-coded:** e.g. statements that apply, main sources of info., important factors in a job, statements that are true etc <u>Hundreds of variations</u>
Do: Behaviours & motivations; Are: Objective characteristics	Open-ended	**No pre-codes or pre-codes:** What like about the employer, what management need to do to improve, why do you agree with statement X etc, <u>Hundreds of variations</u>

Scale questions

Scales are a good way of getting measures of attitudes, opinions, beliefs and behaviour (e.g. frequency) covering many different aspects of the work experience.

Types of scale	Typical wording	Typical Applications
Yes/No	Yes, No	The simplest type of scale. Often used as an alternative to a list to ensure that all items are considered. Can be used to measure knowledge e.g. aware of the following facts, or cultural attributes or presence or absence of individual characteristics.
Agree/disagree	Agree strongly, Tend to agree, Neither, Tend to disagree, Disagree strongly	Used to measure attitudes, opinions to and beliefs about a wide range of aspects of the organisation and employees' experience of working there.
Good/poor	Very good, Fairly good, Neither, Fairly poor, Very poor	Used to rate different facets/experiences of a particular organisation and its practices, e.g. line management, appraisals, the effectiveness of different communications channels, team meetings.

Types of scale	Typical wording	Typical Applications
Satisfaction	Very satisfied, Fairly satisfied, Neither, Fairly dissatisfied, Very dissatisfied	An alternative to the good/poor scale in many cases, though with a slightly different meaning. Perhaps most appropriate for rating different factors in the job or work experience ranging from pay and hours to opportunities for training and development and how staff are treated by line management.
How far applies	Applies strongly, Applies a fair amount, Applies a little, Does not apply at all. A two-point version would be just Applies, Does not apply	Used to explore how far employees feel different attributes apply to their experiences of different aspects of the organisation e.g. the way it treats its staff, communicates, treats customers, its approach to communications, the appraisal system.
Importance	Essential, Very important, Fairly important, Not very important, Not at all important	Used to rate a range of different attributes such as aspects of the job.
Usefulness	Very useful, Fairly useful, Not very useful, Not at all useful	Used to rate particular experiences or services offered e.g. appraisals, communications media like the staff newspaper, intranet or team meetings.
Acceptability	Very acceptable, Fairly acceptable, Neither, Fairly unacceptable, Very unacceptable	Used to rate alternative policies to identify which are most preferred and which are at least acceptable. A better approach than simply asking which are most preferred from a list. Useful for different remuneration packages, modes of communication for particular types of information, terms of employment such as working hours.
Support/oppose	Strongly support, Tend to support, Neither, Tend to oppose, Strongly oppose	Used for measuring opinions on different policies. Can be an alternative to the acceptability scale. Might be applied to proposed policies such as flexitime.
Desirability	Definitely should, Desirable but not essential, Should not	An alternative to support or oppose with a different nuance.

Types of scale	Typical wording	Typical Applications
Better/worse comparisons	A lot better, A little better, About the same, A little worse, A lot worse	Used to compare different experiences over time, e.g. are different aspects of the organisation perceived to have got better or worse, or between environments, e.g. perceived pay and conditions compared with others in the industry.
Meeting expectations	Greatly exceeds my expectations, Somewhat exceeds my expectations, Meets my expectations, Falls somewhat below my expectations, Falls greatly below my expectations	Can be used to see how far various corporate initiatives have delighted or disappointed staff.
Amount	Too much, About the right amount, Too little	Used particularly to explore perceptions of workload e.g. of the employee or their manager. Can also be used for amount of different kinds of information or meetings.
True/False	True, False OR Definitely true, Probably true, Probably false, Definitely false	Used to see the extent to which employees understand, or misunderstand, certain corporate, or other, messages.
Frequency – specific	At least once/week, Less than once/week to once/month, Less than once/month to once/six months, Less often, Never	Used to explore different kinds of behaviour/experiences e.g. how often staff use the company intranet, have a one-to-one with their line manager, an appraisal, team meeting, had difficulty with their IT systems.
Frequency – non-specific	Always, Usually, Occasionally, Never	Used in relation to an event of known frequency that employees may involve themselves with, e.g. readership of the staff newspaper or attendance at a team briefing.
Most recent occurrence	Within the last week, More than a week to one month ago, More than a month to six months ago, Longer ago, Never	Can be alternative to frequency.

Types of scale	Typical wording	Typical Applications
Extent of issue	Major, Minor, None	Sometimes just asking if something is an issue or not is too black and white. Asking if it is a major, minor or no issue at all allows you to focus particularly on things that are regarded as major issues rather than minor irritations.
Numerical	1 to 5, or 1 to 10, or 0 to 10, or -2 to + 2 or -5 to +5	Often used in place of verbal rating scales, but still need to define the meaning of the two extremes e.g. 'excellent' and 'appalling' and maybe the mid-point.

List questions

This technique involves presenting respondents with a list of items and asking them to choose one or more that correspond to their perceptions. Their strength is that they enable you to collect a lot of information very quickly and each item can be compared in terms of frequency of selection with the other items.

You could argue that list questions are the same as scale questions where each item is rated on a one-point scale, or rather two-point scale in that if it is not selected, it might be assumed not to apply. It is often wise to have two questions using the same list asking respondents, for example, firstly which items they feel definitely apply and secondly which definitely do not apply. Those not selected might be categorised as either 'no opinion' or that the respondent feels they 'neither apply nor do not apply' effectively turning the question into a three-point scale question on each item.

Typical applications include:

- Asking respondents to select from a list the factors they consider most important in their job. The same factors can then usefully be rated on a satisfaction or good/poor scale.
- Selecting the types of information they like to receive, perhaps in a grid format by source.
- Selecting adjectives and phrases they think describe the organisation or their department/the way it does things/its culture.
- Statements they believe are true, or false, about the organisation.

- Staff benefits they are aware of/make use of.
- The department/job function/age group/gender/location/ length of service category they belong to.

Open-ended questions

One limitation of pre-coded questions – where the answer has to be selected from a range of given options – is that, respondents have to select the answer that fits closest to what they feel. Open-ended questions, by contrast, can allow respondents to answer in their own words and provide clear pointers towards the issues they believe need to be addressed. However, the answers can only be as good as the questions allow them to be. Moreover, many staff are reluctant to express themselves in this way, especially if writing is not a regular part of their job. Nonetheless, good open-ended questions can provide a much better 'feel' for how the business operates at a cultural level than pre-coded questions, and help to explain the harsher statistical findings. A few open-ended questions should feature in any significant staff survey.

What makes a good employee survey?

A good employee survey will have:

> **A clear purpose** – why it is being conducted, e.g. 'To enable management to understand how far it is delivering on its HR strategy'.
>
> **Clear objectives** – what you want the survey to achieve, e.g. '1. To lay down some key performance indicators that reflect how far we are meeting our strategic HR strategy objectives. 2. To identify issues we need to address to improve organisational performance.
>
> **A clear methodology** – how the survey is to be conducted covering questionnaire design, data collection, data analysis and reporting.

These should all be reflected in the design of the questionnaire so that it covers the right issues, in the right way, is accessible to respondents and is easy for them to complete.

The emergence of agree/disagree scales

The emergence of agree/disagree scales

Origins

Widespread systematic measuring of attitudes using questionnaires is a relatively new thing. Serious interest in the approach grew particularly from the 1920s. The publication of a paper in 1928, by Louis Thurston at the University of Chicago entitled 'Attitudes can be measured' may have marked a watershed in the evolution of the approach that later facilitated the rise of the market and social research industry. He, and later Rensis Likert, became particularly associated with methods, that were named after them, that they developed for measuring attitudes towards different subjects, particularly social issues. Both took the view that to gain an accurate understanding of public opinion on an issue, you needed to measure their views on a number of statements. The first step was therefore to compile a list of statements that reflected the range of more to less extreme opinions on the subject. These were then typically rated by respondents using a balanced positive to negative scale with a neutral point in the middle, e.g. 'strongly agree' to 'strongly disagree' or 'strongly support ' to 'strongly oppose'. To achieve an overall score across all the statements, Thurston would add together the percentages agreeing with each one while Likert allocated scores (e.g. 1 to 5) to each of the scale points the added the scores for each item together.

The method using the latter approach came to be known as the 'Likert scale', the 'scale' being the list of statements that reflected the range of opinions. The term is frequently mistakenly used to refer to the, typically five-point or seven-point, scales used to measure opinions or attitudes on specific items and especially to the agree/disagree scale. This is perhaps understandable as a list of statements does not, on the face it, look like a scale whereas a range of answer categories ranging from very negative to very positive in discrete intervals, does.

Rensis Likert went on to become one of the pioneers of management thinking of the mid-20th century. He ranks alongside the likes of Frederick Herzberg, Douglas McGregor, Abraham Maslow and Elton Mayo as thinkers who changed the way we think about the work place and the role of management in shaping the environments in which we work.

In 1949, he founded the Institute for Social Research at the University of Michigan. He went on to undertake numerous research studies and published two key books on the nature of organisations and management. In this respect, he is probably best known for his idea that there are four systems or styles of management: exploitative authoritarian, benevolent authoritative, consultative and participative group management. According to his research, the most productive is the last of these, participative group management.

However, while the Likert scale is rarely used in commercial research the item scales that he and others developed, have been very widely used not least in the social and market research industries.

Scales used in employee surveys

As we have seen, scales used in questionnaires come in different forms. Generally, though, they fall into three types. There are those that might be called 'zero/positive' scales, those that might be called 'left/right scales' and those that might be called 'positive/negative' scales.

Zero/positive scales are used where you can have gradations of answers but it is not possible to have a negative formulation. For example, they can be useful when measuring behaviours where you may have never done something or may have done it with varying degrees of frequency. Or they can be used to measure awareness or familiarity with something where you may have never heard of it or may know it fairly or very well. Thus, in employee research, you may ask how often, or when was the last time employees have had a one-to-one meeting with their line manager or read the in-house journal and so on. Alternatively, you may ask how well they feel they know the company's goals or objectives with a scale going from 'never heard of' to 'know very well'.

An example of a left/right scale is what is known as a semantic differential scale. Here you are presented with two words or phrases that might be opposites, such as hot/cold, wet/dry, or contrasting, such as traditional/ modern. You are then asked to say whether the object of the research is more like one or more like the other. If the words or statements are clearly meant to convey positive or negative attributes, such as good/bad or attractive/unattractive, then this scale becomes a positive/negative type scale.

Positive/negative scales are used when you are measuring something that can be conceived of in either a positive or a negative way. Thus, it is widely used to measure attitudes and opinions where people can feel either positively or negatively about, for example, various aspects of their workplace or work experience.

These scales can be numerical scales, where you are told what the scale is intended to measure and probably the definition of the end points, e.g. 'excellent' and 'diabolical' or 'extremely satisfied' and 'extremely dissatisfied', and the respondent is asked to give a score from 0 or 1 to maybe 5 or 10 or 100 according to how they think or feel about the item being rated. Alternatively, they may be verbal scales. These are ones where each point on the scale has a verbal tag that tells you what the answer means e.g. 'very good', 'fairly good', etc.

It is these kinds of scales that Thurston and Likert commonly used. The principles underlying these scales are that they should:

- Have a positive end and a negative end with a neutral point in the middle.
- The positive points need to be matched exactly with the equivalent negative points. For example, 'very poor' would pair with 'very good', rather than with 'excellent'.
- Typically the scale will have five points, though it may have more e.g. seven.
- Numerical values can be ascribed to the scale points so long as the positive statements have scores that are equally distant from the mid-point as the equivalent negative statements. Therefore, typically, such scales with five answer categories are scored 1 to 5 with 3 as the mid-point. To reflect the positive/negative nature of the scale these scores are often expressed as going from negative to positive e.g. -2, -1, 0, +1, +2.

The following meet these criteria:

Strongly approve
Tend to approve
Neither approve nor disapprove
Tend to disapprove
Strongly disapprove

and

Very *favourable*
Fairly favourable
Neither favourable nor unfavourable
Fairly unfavourable
Very unfavourable

and

Very good
Fairly good
Neither good nor poor
Fairly poor
Very poor

However, by far the most commonly used variation of such scales is an agree/disagree scale, typically phrased as follows:

Strongly agree
Tend to agree
Neither agree nor disagree
Tend to disagree
Strongly disagree

Many of the largest international consultancies employ surveys consisting of 'agree/disagree' scale questions and virtually nothing else

Perhaps reflecting the particular interest of Rensis Likert and the university of Michigan's Institute for Social Research in organisational psychology, the agree/disagree scale that they widely used has become particularly entrenched in the world of employee research. Indeed, many of the largest international consultancies operating in this area, and many far smaller consultancies, employ surveys that consist of 'agree/disagree' scale questions and, apart from classification questions, virtually nothing else. They include organisations such as Gallup, Best Companies, Watson Wyatt, Towers Perrin/ISR, and ORC.

So, what is the rationale for using only agree/disagree scale questions in an employee survey and what are the particular attractions of the technique?

The attractions of the agree/disagree scale

The way the agree/disagree scale works is that employees are presented with a list of statements about different aspects of their job and the organisation they work for and asked to indicate on a five-, or seven-point, scale how strongly they agree or disagree with each statement.

This approach has several attractions for employee researchers. For one thing, questionnaires using this scale are very easy to construct. You already have the basic question drafted: 'Q How strongly do you agree or disagree with the following statements?' Moreover, you already have the answer categories in the five- or seven-point agree/disagree scale. All you have to do is come up with statements that sound like things staff might say about different aspects of their work experience, then, hey presto, you have your questionnaire!

Questionnaires using this scale are very easy to construct... All you have to do is come up with statements that sound like things staff might say about different aspects of their work experience

Examples of statements used by major consultancies include:

> *'My manager regularly expresses his/her appreciation when I do a good job'*
>
> *'I have access to the training I need in my current position'*
>
> *'My job provides me with an opportunity to use my skills and abilities'*

Sometimes these statements are taken or adapted from discussion groups or interviews with employees. Often they are just made up by the researcher in response to what their clients tell them are the kinds of issues that they wish to explore. Probably most commonly, though, they are simply taken from a database of statements that the research consultancy has used in scores, maybe hundreds, of surveys before.

Typically, these statements will be selected to cover a number of different aspects of the job and working environment. For example: line management, communications, the company's vision or values, training and development, teamwork, job role and pay and benefits.

Another attraction of this technique is that the statements are often relatively easy for respondents to relate to and therefore questionnaires can be completed quite quickly. Once you get the idea that a tick to the right means you agree with the statement and a tick to the left means you disagree, you don't really have to think too much as you read down the page ticking the boxes.

The statements are often relatively easy for respondents to relate to... they don't really have to think too much as they read down the page ticking the boxes

A further attraction for employee research consultants is the fact that numerical scores can be attributed to each of the points on the scale and that the range of scores is identical for every statement. This makes the data very amenable to various kinds of statistical, especially multivariate, analysis. If you think of each statement as a separate variable, each time a respondent answers a question they are providing a numerical score. This score can then be used to relate the different variables together to see, for example, how far a high score on one variable tends to occur (or is correlated) with a high score on other variables. Statisticians love that sort of thing!

Finally, agree/disagree scales are attractive to consultants as they lend themselves to compiling normative databases. Many leading employee research consultancies require you to use their standard statements. In that way, they are able to build up a large database of 'norms' – i.e. the results from the same statements put to employees in lots of different

Consultants like agree/disagree scales as they lend themselves to compiling normative databases

organisations. They can then tell you whether responses in your organisation are better or worse than the average of all the organisations they have used the statements in, and sometimes organisations in your sector or region as well.

Although these may all seem like benefits of using agree/disagree scale questions in an employee survey, as we shall see later, they also come at a cost; the cost is that you are not necessarily asking the questions that best suit your organisation.

When should you use the agree/disagree scale?

The agree/disagree scale is mainly used for measuring employees' attitudes, opinions and beliefs. It is worth reflecting on the difference between these. In reality, though, it can be difficult to define whether a particular statement is measuring an attitude, an opinion or a belief. Take the statement: '*I have confidence in the senior management of [Employer] to lead us in the right direction*'. Is this measuring an opinion – the opinion that senior management are leading us in the right direction – an attitude - a positive feeling of trust in the top management – or a belief – a belief that senior management is leading the business in the right direction? In reality, probably all three.

However, although they can overlap, it is probably useful to make the distinction. Attitudes are generally taken to be emotionally charged and may not have a substantial basis. Opinions tend to be judgmental – this or that is a good policy, should or should not be done. Beliefs are about what you believe to be true though there are different kinds. Some might be said to be 'cognitive beliefs' – things you have learnt to be true and which might be supported by what you would regard as concrete evidence – e.g. senior management said they would take certain steps that would improve the organisation and you have seen this happen. Then there are what might be called 'faith beliefs' – there may not be any substantial evidence, but you believe something to be true because you want to, maybe because you trust the source of the belief. For example, you may want to believe that senior management are leading the business in the right direction and you feel positive towards them and trust them to do what is right, even though, as yet, there is no evidence to support their claims. Then there are what might be called 'conviction beliefs'. These are beliefs about what ought to be the case and may well reflect your own personal religious, moral or political values.

Most 'employee attitude' surveys in reality measure a combination of attitudes, opinions and the different kinds of beliefs. The agree/disagree scale is probably most useful for measuring employees' beliefs. If management think that the success of the organisation depends, in part at least, in employees believing certain things about their job or the organisation, the technique can be used to test the hypothesis that this is the case.

For example, in one organisation, which had particular performance problems, we wanted to see if staff believed that it was capable of improving. The statement: *'I believe (Employer) can significantly improve its performance'* provided welcome reassurance that deep down people believed that great things were possible.

The agree/ disagree scale is probably most useful for measuring employees' beliefs

In another organisation, I designed a questionnaire that contained a number of untried questions so a pilot was conducted among a small number of employees selected from across the organisation. The questionnaire contained a section where staff were asked to rate their line manager on various specific criteria. Having done so, one respondent remarked that the apparently poor performance was not actually her line manager's fault. In her view, the line managers in her department were all overworked. This led us to include a question that allowed us to test the hypothesis that many managers throughout the organisation were believed to have too much to do and that this affected their ability to do their work properly. The hypothesis was confirmed and provided a very different perspective on the research findings than would otherwise have been the case.

In another organisation, the client had a number of specific hypotheses relating to the appraisal system and how it was working. A series of agree/disagree scale statements seemed the best way to test these hypotheses. Thus, among the statements we included were:

'The nature of my role means that even if I carry out my duties to the highest standard, I am unable to meet the definition of a 'top performer''

'I feel that I can be rewarded fairly as a result of the appraisal process'

'The appraisal process relies too heavily on the subjective views of my line manager'

'The scoring system used in the appraisals is generally fair'

Some statements can be useful as overall measures of commitment, pride or the strength of the internal culture. For example:

'I feel proud to work for [Employer]'

'I would recommend [Employer] as a place to work'

Mostly, though, the rationale for using agree/disagree scale questions is that they 'map out' different facets of the culture of an organisation – 'the way things are done around here'. Arguably, they enable you to get a feel for the organisation and what it is like working for it.

In one organisation, we found that fewer than half agreed that: *'I feel I belong here'*, which was quite a shattering revelation for senior management. In another, we found over 50% agreed with the statement that *'Speaking up on issues where you disagree with management can severely damage your career prospects'*. Widespread agreement with such a statement indicates a culture of blame and intimidation, which is unlikely to realise the full potential of individuals or the organisation as a whole.

Mostly, the rationale for using agree/disagree scale questions is that they 'map out' different facets of the culture

Typically, surveys consisting (almost) exclusively of agree/disagree scale questions have a handful - perhaps between two and eight - statements about each of a number of different facets of the organisation e.g. line management, communications, training and development, the job and so on. Here are the statements one major consultancy uses to measure attitudes to personal development, for example:

'I am a satisfied with the chance I have to use my skills in my job'

'I have access to the training I need to be productive in my current position'

'My team leader coaches me to improve my performance'

'My team leader does a good job of assessing my strengths and personal development needs'

If you read the answers to such statements, you will form a number of impressions of what it is like working there from a personal development point of view. Thus, widespread agreement with *'I am satisfied with the chance I have to use my skills in my job'* might give you an impression of contented staff that have been recruited into jobs for which they are well suited. Widespread disagreement might give you an impression of staff who are frustrated because the organisation requires them to do things that they are ill-suited to, bored by and would rather not do. Widespread agreement with *'My team leader does a good job of assessing my strengths and personal development needs'* might give you an impression of line management that undertakes frequent one-to-one meetings, are always looking for opportunities to develop the skills of their staff and that play to their strengths. Widespread disagreement might give you an impression of managers who generally ignore the needs of their staff and pile work on them irrespective of where their capabilities lie and with no interest in their long-term development.

You might then take these four statements as a whole to build a fuller picture of how staff experience personal development in the organisation. You might then take the answers to all the other statements used to measure your employees' attitudes to the other facets of the organisation to build up a more complete picture of what it is like working there.

If the agree/disagree scale is the only tool used in your employee survey, you will be excluded from understanding many of the things that are most critical in managing your organisation's performance

This is essentially what most consultancies that undertake surveys based on agree/disagree scales do. Often they are called 'cultural audits'. The idea is that by measuring agreement with lots of different statements drafted to reflect the kinds of things people might think or feel about their job and working environment), you can build up a picture of the key aspects that define its culture. The underlying assumption is often that it is the culture – particularly how well staff are motivated and how they relate to their working environment – that ultimately drives the organisation's performance.

There is undoubtedly something in this, so it is important to acknowledge that the agree/disagree scale has a role to play in employee surveys. However, the agree/disagree scale approach has significant limitations and if it is the only tool used in your employee survey, you will be excluded from understanding many of the things that are most critical in managing your organisation's performance.

PART 2

The limitations of the agree/disagree scale

PART 2: The limitations of the agree/disagree scale

What is wrong with the agree/disagree scale?

You might argue that most statements used in agree/disagree scales fall into the category I have described as 'hypothesis testing' i.e. they are testing hypotheses about the way people think about their job/work environment. For example, here is a selection of statements taken from the surveys of a number of different consultancies.

'I am satisfied about where the organisation is going'

'The decisions senior managers make concerning employees are usually fair'

'I am happy with the balance between my home and work life'

'The training in my job is of great benefit to me personally'

'I believe that progression and promotion decisions at this company are fair and objective'

'I am kept well informed about what is happening in [Employer]'

'Overall, I think I am paid fairly compared with people in [Employer] who are in similar jobs'

'I feel I can make a difference in this organisation'

All of these, you might say, test hypotheses. *'I am satisfied about where the organisation is going'*, for example, might be said to be testing the hypothesis that most staff feel they know where the organisation is going; and presumably someone in the organisation believes that it is important for the success of the organisation that staff do believe that they know where it is going. The statement *'I feel I can make a difference in this organisation'* might be said to be testing the hypothesis that the staff feel empowered.

But are they really doing that? The rest of this section explores some of the limitations of agree/disagree scale questions.

Vague and impressionistic

If you reflect on these kinds of statements (listed above), two things might strike you. The first is that they are all somewhat vague. In other words, they tend to point you towards a particular issue without being too specific about how that issue manifests itself in your particular organisation. There is a very good reason for that. If you use a consultancy that has its own standard set of attitude statements, then the statements were never actually developed for *your* organisation in the first place. Rather, they were developed so that they made some kind of sense in *any* organisation, but not so that they made very profound sense in any *particular* organisation. Because the statements are somewhat vague then what you are measuring is also somewhat vague and impressionistic. That is what the agree/disagree scale used in most employee surveys does; it measures general impressions people have about their work and the organisation they work in.

These kinds of statements were developed so that they made some kind of sense in <u>any</u> organisation, not so that they made very profound sense in <u>any particular</u> organisation

You often do not know what is in respondents' minds

The second thing that might strike you is that it is often very difficult to interpret what the answers to the statements mean. Let us take the statement '*I am satisfied about where the organisation is going*'. Since you do not know what is in respondents' minds when they are answering the question, you have no idea what agreement means – do they actually know where their organisation is going and share the same notion as senior management or do they just have a general impression of knowing where it is going?

It is often very difficult to interpret what the answers to the statements mean

Because the statements are so often stated in rather general terms, it is easy for employees to associate *some kind* of meaning to each statement. However, that is not to say that everyone attributes the *same* meaning to each statement. Moreover, there is a tendency when looking at the results to project your own prejudices on to the questions and the interpretation of them. If people share your view, you will tend to assume they do so for the same reasons as you do, for example.

This happens to some extent with all attitude statements, but the more generalised and vague they are, the more vulnerable they are to a multiplicity of interpretations, which renders them either in-actionable or vulnerable to being grossly misinterpreted.

Open-ended questions, or other kinds of exploratory research, can often reveal a wide range of feelings, views and experiences lying behind any particular attitude. If we take the statement *'I intend to be working for the company in 12 months' time'*, for example, a quick reading of the results would suggest that those who agree are somehow more committed, loyal and motivated than those who disagree. Indeed one consultancy uses this as a key measure of employee engagement. However, if we probe on this question, we would realise that there are many reasons why employees could disagree, but still be very loyal. For example, they may be leaving to retire, start a family or move away with a partner or spouse. Or they may agree, but not be particularly loyal or committed. For example, the job may be conveniently located, they may believe they would find it hard to find another job or they may feel that the pay is good, even though they dislike the work, and so on.

Of course, you cannot ask an open-ended question after every agree/disagree scale statement. You are thus, sadly, left with a large number of responses that may suggest you have issues you need to deal with but precious little insight into what those issues are!

It is often particularly difficult to know what disagreement with a particular statement means

While agreement with positive statements is generally reassuring, problems often arise with understanding what *disagreement* with those statements mean. In the example cited above – *'I am satisfied about where the organisation is going'* - does disagreement mean that employees think they know where the organisation is going but are dissatisfied with that direction, or do they just have no idea of where it is going? High neutral responses may also indicate that staff do not feel they know where the organisation is going or that they find the statement so vague that they are not clear what it is supposed to mean!

Responses to agree/disagree statements are often misinterpreted because it is not clear whether disagreement with a statement means agreement with the opposite of that statement or something else. Indeed, it is often unclear what the opposite of the statement would be. For example, if staff disagree with the statement: *'I believe management has a clear vision for the future'*, does that mean they think management has an *un*clear vision for the future, or does it mean that they believe management has *no* vision for the future, or perhaps it means that they *don't know* if management has a clear vision or not?

It would be better to formulate the question as follows:

Q Which of these statements comes closest to your view of top management's vision for the future of the business?

They have a very clear vision

They have a vision, but it is not very clear

They have no vision at all

I do not know if they have a vision or not

There are hundreds of other examples that could be cited. For example, does disagreement with the statement: *'I fully support the values for which [Employer] stands'* mean that they oppose the values, that they do not know what the values are or that they support them to some extent but not fully?

Because the statement is so unspecific, if people disagree with it we have no idea what is in their mind

What does disagreement with: *'I am kept well informed about what is happening in [Employer]'*, mean? We really have no idea since the statement is so unspecific. Are staff thinking about information about their department or their division or the company as a whole? Are they referring to information to do with commercial performance or strategic plans or new product development or restructuring and redundancies or job and training opportunities? The trouble is that such generalised statements provide no specific information to which management can respond to improve the situation.

Poor at capturing the complexity of organisations

Agree/disagree scale questions are generally poor at capturing the complexity of how organisations work. Take communications, for example. Typically, when agree/disagree scales are applied to explore communications within an organisation, the statements used are largely bland and meaningless. Here are some examples used by major consultancies:

Agree/disagree scale questions are generally poor at capturing the complexity of how organisations work

'My information needs are well met'

'I rely on my manager to give me information to do my job'

'Regular updates from my manager are useful at telling me what is happening'

'My manager and I communicate effectively with each other'

'Communications are good in this company/my department'

'We receive information in a timely manner'

The fact is there is very little you can do with the answers that such questions generate. For example, when people disagree with the statement *'Communications are good in this company/my department'* you are given no insight into the nature of any issues the company needs to address. Is it that little communication appears to happen? Or does it happen but is not believed? Or does it come via the

Typically, when agree/disagree scales are applied to explore communications, the statements used are largely bland and meaningless... There is very little you can do with the answers that such questions generate

wrong channels? Or is the information delivered too late, or what? It just fails to shed any light on what specifically is poor about the communications.

Here, open-ended questions might help in identifying the issues that lie behind the attitudes. However, it is often better to break down communications into different types and explore them separately rather than lump them all in together. Different kinds of information are communicated in any organisation. However, most of this information tends to fall into the following four categories:

1) Information employees need to do their jobs on a day-to-day basis
2) Information/feedback on how they are doing in their job
3) Information about how the organisation as a whole/their division/department is doing
4) Information about things that are going on in the organisation generally.

Each of these is quite different. Now, at least, you can focus on each one, perhaps rating them in terms of how well staff feel their needs are met in each area. Far better than asking how strongly they agree or disagree that: *'My information needs are well met'* when you have no idea what kind of information needs they are thinking of.

Because agree/disagree scale questions are so bad at grasping the complexity of the workplace, there is a grave danger that they will be misinterpreted. For example, if you take the statement *'I rely on my manager to give me information to do my job'*, there is a strong likelihood that a high level of disagreement will be interpreted as managers not doing their job properly. But what if the employees do not look to their manager to give them information to do their job and the manager does not expect them to? What if staff are quite happy to seek out the information they need from colleagues, the intranet, industry or other sources to get the information they need? Rather than reflecting a poorly managed, dysfunctional organisation, high levels of disagreement may actually reflect a highly empowered and effective organisation!

There is also an assumption that people want to be communicated with and that communication is always a good thing. In reality, people often complain about information overload. What they really want is the right kind of information through, what they would regard as, the most appropriate channels.

Many questions also make the mistake of assuming that communication is a one-way process, normally from management to staff. These assumptions may well have been how it generally worked many decades ago, when staff were expected to be far more deferential to management and before technology increased the amount and accessibility of information a thousand-fold. However, staff are now far more empowered to access information and are expected to make judgements about what information they need. Questions that explore communications systems need to reflect this.

Many questions make the mistake of assuming that communication is a one-way process, normally from management to staff

Lists and scales that correspond to how people actually relate to different kinds of information and channels will enable you to capture this complexity and draw valid conclusions from the results. For example, in a survey for a major healthcare organisation, I developed two questions in a grid format. The first grid listed different types of information and we asked staff to say whether they were *'interested in it and received it'*, were *'interested and knew where to get it if they wanted it'*, were *'interested but did not know where to get it'* were *'not interested but received it anyway'* and were *'not interested and did not get it'*.

Q Below is a list of areas of news and information about Co A. Please indicate how you feel about each one.

Answer categories	Items evaluated
I am interested in it and receive it	*a) The annual financial results of Co A*
I am interested in it and know where to get it if I want it	*b) Updates of how the business you work in is doing throughout the year*
I am interested in it and do not know where to get it	*c) People leaving or joining your area of the business*
I am not interested in it even though I receive it	*d) Regular (e.g. weekly) news updates and information about my place of work etc*
I am not interested in it and do not receive it	

In the next question, we explored, for the same list of items, via which channel or channels they would most prefer to receive the information. It may sound complicated, but because the information items and channels were ones that staff were familiar with, the questions worked well.

Q Below is a list of channels through which you could receive each item of information. Please indicate which channel or channels you prefer to use for each type of information.

Answer categories	Items evaluated
The company intranet	*a) The annual financial results of Co A*
The company's website	*b) Updates of how the business you work in is doing throughout the year*
Notice boards	*c) People leaving or joining your area of the business*
Face-to- face e.g. briefings, team meetings	*d)Regular (e.g. weekly) news updates and information about my place of work*
Email	*etc*
Staff news-paper etc	

Right issues, wrong format

The agree/disagree scale is, of course, only one type of scale that can be used to measure attitudes. Many consultancies use it exclusively because the consistency of the scale is necessary for their statistical multivariate analyses to work. If they decide that a particular issue needs to be covered, a question has to be phrased so that it fits into the agree/disagree scale format. A lot of the time, though, this is just not the best question format to use.

Consultancies often exclusively use the agree/disagree scale because the consistency of the scale is necessary for their statistical multivariate analyses to work

One major healthcare company, for example, was considering different ways of delivering its employee newspaper. It was interested in staff attitudes to the different options. We could have asked a series of agree/disagree questions along the lines of:

Q How strongly do you agree or disagree that:

'I would find it acceptable if the (Staff Newspaper) was delivered by post to my home'

'I would find it acceptable if the (Staff Newspaper) was delivered through collection points in my office'

'I would find it acceptable if the (Staff Newspaper) was delivered to my desk or pigeon hole'

And so on.

That would have worked but, as the issue was all about the acceptability of different options, we opted for a five-point acceptability scale ranging from 'very acceptable' to 'very unacceptable'.

Questions like this make the questionnaire much more focused on producing actionable results. Questionnaires that list dozens of statements against the one agree/disagree scale are necessarily constrained in what they can ask. It makes sense to break the questions up into sections within the questionnaire, but it also makes sense to consider what the best question format is for the issues you are addressing.

Questionnaires that list dozens of statements against the one agree/disagree scale are necessarily constrained in what they can ask

Most general employee survey questionnaires will include questions designed to measure how employees feel about line management. Here are some of the statements that major consultancies use in their surveys:

'My manager regularly expresses his/her appreciation when I do a good job'

'My manager is good at motivating me to do the best I can at work'

'I feel that my manager talks openly and honestly with me'

Again, an agree/disagree scale works, but so too does a scale that asks employees to rate their immediate line manager in terms of how good or poor they are – using a five-point 'very good' to 'very poor' scale - in each respect. In fact, such a scale works better because it is more in line with how employees think about their managers. You can also introduce the subject and focus on all the different aspects that you want to explore. Thus, you might ask: *'How would you rate your immediate line manager in terms of each of the following?'* You can then list all the key management behaviours that you are aiming to encourage within the organisation and do not need to keep repeating *'My manager'* in every statement.

A five- point 'very good' to 'very poor' scale works better because it is more in line with how employees think about their managers

Because you are using a consistent scale, the responses on each item can be compared with all the other items. Despite what some consultants might infer, there is just no need to compare staff responses to the questions on line management with their responses to the questions on other aspects of working in the organisation such as internal communication or remuneration. They therefore do not need to be confined to using just one type of scale

One the most useful attitudinal questions you can ask in employee surveys is how staff feel about the different aspects of their job. In most organisations, you can compile a list of between twenty and thirty items that it is reasonable to assume employees value, to varying degrees, in their job. These are likely to include things like overall remuneration, how they are treated by line management, opportunities for career development, the physical working environment, interesting work and so on. However, to list these in an agree/disagree format becomes nonsensical. Imagine if you had a questionnaire where there were twenty statements along the lines:

'I am satisfied with my overall pay'

'I am satisfied with the way I am treated by my line manager'

'I am satisfied with how interesting my work is'

'I am satisfied with the opportunities I have for career development'

It quickly becomes apparent that the statements seem repetitive and awkward. It should also become apparent that this is the wrong way to ask these questions. Instead of forcing the items into an agree/disagree format, you should list out the items against a satisfaction scale such as: *'very satisfied, fairly satisfied, neither, fairly dissatisfied, very dissatisfied'*. If you do this you then realise that there are far more things that matter to employees than are reflected in questionnaires that rely solely on agree/disagree scales. However, because forcing them into the agree/disagree format looks awkward and contrived, most of these things are omitted. It is a characteristic of that question technique that it is unsuited to, and therefore fails to capture, what employees value most in their jobs day-to-day.

No facility for prioritisation of issues

This example flags another major limitation of agree/disagree scales used without the support of other questions: they provide no facility for respondents to prioritise the issues in terms of their importance. Even if they did, in this question format the answers would be nonsensical. It makes sense to have a question asking staff to say what issues they think the business should prioritise, but not which of a list of attitudes are most important to address.

In lieu of any indication of what staff believe it is most important to address, most attention is often focused on the positive statements with the lowest level of agreement (or the negative statements with the highest level of agreement) and/or the ones that score least well relative to the consultancies' norms. The trouble with this is that, whether staff agree or disagree with a statement, it does not mean that they necessarily care much about the issue covered. In reality, some of these attitudes could reflect quite trivial issues, while others reflect much more profound issues. For example, if we take the statements above about line management, it may well be that staff value greatly their manager being 'open and honest' with them, but do not care too much if their manager does not express appreciation for their work on a regular basis.

Developed essentially to measure attitudes and opinions

Thus, the agree/disagree scale is not the only way to measure staff attitudes and frequently not the most appropriate way either. However, there are a large number of other reasons why the agree/disagree scale fails to deliver what management really needs, and should expect from, its employee surveys. These have to do with the fact that the scale was developed essentially to measure attitudes and opinions, though it is also useful for measuring beliefs. It was never intended to measure aspects of people's jobs and their working environment that are equally accessible through survey research and at least as important to understand as *attitudes* if you are aiming to improve the experience of your employees and the performance of your organisation. These are people's *behaviours, motivations,* and *knowledge.*

Inappropriate for measuring behaviours

It is often very helpful to know how people are behaving in your organisation. In communications, for example, it can be very useful to know how often people use various channels. However, statements like:

> *'I rely on my manager to give me information to do my job'*
>
> *'We have regular team briefings in my area'*
>
> *'I use the intranet when I need information'*

are next to useless. A scaled question exploring how frequently a list of channels are used by different members of staff, is far more enlightening and can incorporate an option for 'not aware of' the channel. For example:

Q Which category most closely describes how often you do/take part in each of the following?

Answer categories	Items evaluated
Daily	*a) Attend a team briefing*
Weekly	*b) Look at the company intranet*
Every 2 weeks	*c) Look at the company website*
Monthly	*d) Look at notice boards*
Less often	etc
Never	
Not aware of	

Unlike the attitude statements, this question provides hard behavioural information on usage and enables direct comparisons to be made between channels. A more sophisticated version would identify preferred channels for different kinds of information.

Unable to explain behaviours

There is often an assumption that attitudes drive behaviours and that if people have negative attitudes they will therefore behave in a negative way. This may be true and there is at least an implicit assumption in those consultancies that only measure attitudes in their surveys that this is the case; change the attitudes and you change the behaviours. The problem is knowing which of the attitudes measured in the survey affect which behaviours. Questionnaires that consist of only agree/disagree statements measuring attitudes give you no insight into this at all.

However, questionnaires that include behavioural questions as well as agree/disagree statements still do not allow you to match one against the other to understand what is driving what. Although you can cross-tabulate behavioural questions by attitudinal questions or use regression analysis (see section below) to see what attitudinal variables appear to correlate with the behavioural variables, at best this can be broadly indicative that the two variables are linked, at worst it can provide you with a wholly misleading steer.

The fact is, attitudes do not really drive behaviours. However, feelings and beliefs, that attitudes often reflect, can do, although one feeling or belief can give rise to an enormously wide range of attitudes, and behaviours. They are both, if you like symptoms not causes.

The fact is, attitudes do not really drive behaviours

Behaviours are really what drive performance in organisations. In order to change behaviours, you really need to understand what is motivating staff to behave in a particular way and, equally important, what is stopping them behaving in the way in which you require them to.

Because agree/disagree scale statements can only measure one thing at a time, they are really rather poor at this. For example, if you wanted to know why people do not attend team meetings, it would be a cumbersome approach to go through a list of reasons why they may not attend asking how strongly they agreed or disagreed that *'I don't attend team meetings because I am not informed when they occur'* or *'I do not attend team meetings because they do not discuss things that I am interested in'* and so on. A far better approach would be a list question along the lines of:

> *Q Which, if any, of these reasons best explain why you do not attend team meetings?*

then to list the possible reasons. By having this question follow on immediately after the behavioural question asking about their attendance at team meetings (for example) it is already directly linked to the behaviour you are trying to explain.

Although some consultancies try to explain behaviours using multiple regression analysis, as I explain elsewhere, this can be dangerously misleading. The best way to find out why people behave in a certain way is generally to ask them a straight and objective question, not to try to derive it by seeing how far their answers correlate statistically with other questions in the questionnaire.

Failure to evaluate what people know and test assumptions

What people know, or believe they know, about an organisation is a critical aspect of the way they engage with it. Yet agree/disagree statements are frequently phrased in such a way as to ignore the possibility that staff simply do not know to what they refer. For example, it is not uncommon to see statements like the following used to explore how employees feel about their employer's vision, mission, values or objectives:

Statements are frequently phrased in such a way as to ignore the possibility that staff simply do not know to what they refer

> *'I believe strongly in the goals and objectives of (Employer)'*
>
> *'I fully support the values for which (Employer) stands'*
>
> *'I believe top management has a clear vision for the future'*
>
> *'I understand (employer's) strategic direction and objectives'*

The trouble is, these are management concepts and many staff will not necessarily understand the terms 'mission', 'vision', 'values' or 'objectives'. Moreover, they can easily be confused between group, corporate, divisional, departmental and individual objectives and goals. Using statements such as:

'I am aware of [Employer's] core values and purpose'

'I am aware of [Employer's] strategy and goals'

does not help the situation. Far better to state what it is you are talking about e.g. the actual corporate vision/values/objectives, then ask questions about them that you know cannot be confused. Thus, you can explore if they are aware of them, if they buy into them, if they feel management lives up to them, if they believe they are achievable, what they consider to be the main barriers to their realisation and so on. All these questions will provide far more insight into how the core management thinking really works throughout the organisation than the agree/disagree scale responses. The information will also be far more actionable.

Basic awareness is often a very good reason why people do not engage with different facets of the business. It might be awareness of a whole host of things such as core management thinking and policy, key policies and practices such as appraisal systems and training programmes, remuneration packages and bonus package options, job opportunities or plans for the business.

Simple list questions asking which items staff are aware of will paint a much clearer picture of how engaged they are with key aspects of the organisation

Simple list questions asking which they are aware of will paint a much clearer picture of how engaged staff are with key aspects of the organisation. Various scale questions providing gradations of awareness – e.g. 'fully aware, partially aware, heard of but know hardly anything about' and 'never heard of' - can provide a more subtle understanding

Prevent staff from providing considered responses

The use of the agree/disagree scale in employee surveys is often defended on the grounds that it is easy for the staff to complete; they do not have to think too much, just read the statement and tick a box. However, to my mind, that somewhat defeats the object of asking your employees for their views. Surely, you want them to think about their answers, often quite deeply. In this way, you will get more considered, reflective and valuable responses that you can draw on to improve the organisation and its performance.

The agree/disagree scale is often defended on the grounds that staff do not have to think too much. To my mind, that defeats the object of asking for their views

How the use of agree/disagree scales has evolved

It is curious that, although the founding fathers of empirical organisational research used a wide range of questioning techniques, just one kind of question technique should have become so entrenched in many of the leading commercial organisations undertaking employee surveys.

One of the best known of these was Rensis Likert, who ran the Institute for Social Research at the University of Michigan from 1949 until 1969. During that time, he wrote two important books 'New Patterns in Management' (1961) and 'The Human Organisation: Its Management and Value' (1967). He also undertook a great deal of empirical research among employees of different organisations. For this, he used a very wide range of questions – lists, open-ended questions, balanced and non-balanced scales.

What seems to have happened over the last forty years or so is that two traditions have defined the way in which questionnaires have been constructed for employee surveys. There is what I would call the 'market research tradition' where a range of different questioning techniques are applied to capture different aspects of the internal culture – attitudes, opinions, beliefs, behaviours, preferences, motivations, knowledge and so on. This is consistent with what market researchers do in their mainstream activities, using surveys to understand what people think and feel about products or advertising and how they behave as consumers.

The 'agree/disagree scale tradition' has settled on the idea that the only thing that matters is staff attitudes/opinions and the only way to measure these is using an agree/disagree scale

Then there is the 'agree/disagree scale tradition' that has settled on the idea that the only thing that matters is staff attitudes/opinions and the only way to measure these is using an agree/disagree scale. Some consultancies have defaulted to a standard set of statements that they insist on asking in every organisation irrespective of those organisations' individual needs.

Perhaps because employee research was, and remains, very marginal to the mainstream market research industry, it seems to have allowed consultants that come from different traditions of thinking, rooted in management consulting, organisational change and recruitment, to take a lead in this area.

How employee survey formats have evolved

Agree/disagree scale tradition

'Attitude' scales invented → Agree/disagree scale only questions; Mainly agree/disagree scale, some others; Some agree/disagree scale, mainly others

Agree/disagree scale only questions → All standardised statements; Mix of standard and non-standard statements; No standardised statements (rare)

All standardised statements → No customisation

Mix of standard and non-standard statements → Some customisation

Mainly agree/disagree scale, some others → Some customisation

No standardised statements (rare) → Highly customisable survey

Some agree/disagree scale, mainly others → Highly customisable survey

No agree/disagree scale questions → Highly customisable survey

Market research tradition

But why did these consultants latch so firmly onto the agree/disagree scale technique to the virtual exclusion of all other techniques?

There are probably a number of reasons. The first is that their core business was generally not (market) research. The (market) research industry, by and large, makes money by delivering information about what people think, feel and do and why. Questionnaire design is a core and very necessary skill. It requires a lot of practice and training and a particular kind of analytical mind. This is not normally a core skill for consultancies, especially ones where employee surveys constitute a tiny part of their overall revenue. The consultants' mindset is more likely 'top down' than 'bottom up' with the focus more on numbers they can compute than insights that might challenge their models. Consultants like numbers and especially numbers that support their theories of how organisations work or perhaps that support the other services they are selling! The agree/disagree scale requires very little questionnaire design skill; all you do is make up statements about different aspects of the job and work environment.

Moreover, if your consultancy has defaulted to a standard set of statements then you need no questionnaire design skills at all!

For those that prefer to retain some ability to adapt the questionnaire to their individual clients' needs, the agree/disagree format provides a lot of flexibility. There is no end to the number of statements that you can squeeze into the format covering an enormously wide range of attitudes. It is not bound by any particular context so within the same format you can ask questions about management, communications, pay, work relations, work-life balance and so on.

Moreover, it produces a lot of numbers. For researchers, the numbers are usually the main output. For many consultants, they are the starting point for 'adding value'. In some cases, this can involve multivariate analysis that has the air of scientific sophistication for which some can charge handsomely, even though, as we shall see, the findings are often spurious. In other cases, this involves a range of consultancy services designed to achieve various cultural, organisational or leadership objectives. The attitude statements can usually be relied on to identify a large number of issues that can benefit from such services.

The apparently unquestioning way in which these consultancies have adopted the agree/disagree scale approach is summed up by the Best Companies [2] organisation. In explaining its rationale for adopting the technique, it references 'The Survey Research Handbook' by Alreck and Settle[3] in listing the following 'advantages' of the scale:

Power - The scaled response gives granular data in a powerful format for analysis.

Simplicity for respondent – The response scale is consistent and understandable no matter what the question type and there are no complex instructions for completing the survey.

Flexibility – The statement format of questions does not restrict the type of question that can be asked.

Economy – Question statements can be short and to the point.

Comparability – All responses are on the same scale and thus directly comparable statistically.

Summated values – While the response scale is strictly categorical in nature, it does have a clear scale value of increasing positivity and thus score values can be summed or averaged across respondents.

Years of background research – As the standard survey method in the social sciences, the issues with statistical analysis and validity of results are very well known.

The irony is that *none* of these 'advantages' uniquely apply to the agree/disagree scale and several are just basically wrong! The following table reviews each 'advantage' in turn.

The irony is that none of these 'advantages' uniquely apply to the agree/disagree scale and several are just basically wrong!

'Advantages' of the agree/disagree scale	Comment
Power - The scaled response gives granular data in a powerful format for analysis.	So can any scale, whether used for measuring attitudes or not.
Simplicity for respondent – The response scale is consistent and understandable no matter what the question type and there are no complex instructions for completing the survey.	Good researchers always aim to make *any* survey question understandable and avoid complex instructions. Other scales can also be applied to a list of statements thereby being 'consistent'.
Flexibility – The statement format of questions does not restrict the type of question that can be asked.	Actually, it very much restricts the type of questions that can be asked. The fact is that if you confine yourself to the agree/disagree scale, as Best Companies has, then only questions that can be phrased in an agree/disagree statement format can be included.
Economy – Question statements can be short and to the point.	It is good practice to try to make *all* survey questions focused and to the point, including, for example, items in lists.

'Advantages' of the agree/disagree scale	Comment
Comparability – All responses are on the same scale and thus directly comparable statistically.	It is unclear what being 'directly comparable statistically' means in this context. The author probably means that the responses can be converted into scores (e.g. strongly disagree=1 to strongly agree =5) and then used in multivariate analysis. However, in other ways, the responses are really not very comparable. Respondents are not, for example, asked to rate a list of items (e.g. their line manager's behaviours) for how good/poor they are or to select items from a list (e.g. preferred communications channels), which would allow statements to be compared. The thing about attitudes is that comparing one with another generally does not make much sense.
Summated values – While the response scale is strictly categorical in nature, it does have a clear scale value of increasing positivity and thus score values can be summed or averaged across respondents.	This is true for other scales, so does not justify the use only of the agree/disagree scale.
Years of background research – As the standard survey method in the social sciences the issues with statistical analysis and validity of results are very well known.	Unfortunately most of this 'background research' has been about whether the answers achieved are different from what you would expect if people just selected answers at random or whether it is better to use a 4,5,7,9 or 11-point scale. It has not been about whether the technique is actually the most appropriate to use in surveys designed to help you manage your business.

The list reads like a post hoc rationalisation of the technique they had already settled on. There is no evidence that the Best Company researchers seriously considered using any other question types.

Of course, once you have settled on just using the agree/disagree scale there are hundreds, even thousands, of different attitudes that you can measure. As more and more issues are raised, the natural reaction is to draft more and more statements to capture each attitude. You can easily end up with literally hundreds of statements in any one questionnaire, which become both tedious for the respondents and unwieldy to make sense of. Yet, this is what some consultancies offer.

This approach would be in keeping with the way Rensis Likert and others in his tradition saw these types of scale being used. His idea was to take an issue and to list out lots of statements some supporting one side of an argument, others supporting another side, so that you build up a picture of the range and types of feelings people have about it. Of course, in a complex organisation you are likely to want to explore many different issues in lots of different areas – management style, training, communications, etc. It is logical, then, to go on creating more and more statements in order to cover off as many aspects of the work experience as you can.

The trouble is you end up with hundreds of measures and it quickly becomes mind numbing and, in managerial terms, unusable.

While some consultancies still churn out surveys consisting of, in some cases, over 200 agree/disagree statements, most have taken a more disciplined approach and culled these down to a more manageable number – perhaps sixty or seventy organised under different themes with, perhaps, between three and eight statements under each theme.

You end up with hundreds of measures and it quickly becomes mind numbing and, in managerial terms, unusable

Moreover, often these statements will have been standardised. In other words, exactly the same statements will be asked about training or management or communications in each organisation irrespective of how training, management or communications are actually carried out in those organisations.

The consultancies' justification for this is that you can then compare your results with the highest, lowest and average scores found across all the other companies where the same questions have been asked. Some consultancies will only allow their standardised questions to be asked so that your results can be compared with their norms. However, this may not necessarily be as beneficial as it may at first seem!

The Nonsense of Norms

Asking exactly the same questions in your organisation as the consultant has asked in lots of other organisations so that you can compare your results with their average, or normative, responses, may initially sound like a major benefit. If you can overlook the fact that none of the questions has specifically been developed to meet the needs of your business, at least you can see whether your scores are good, average or poor relative to other organisations. The implication is that you should focus on those areas where your company scores relatively poorly against the norms. However, there is a price to pay.

Are you being distracted from your true purpose?

There is one very practical drawback to a norms-driven approach to employee surveys, particularly if the norms are very specific measures. Increasingly, norms have been presented as Key Performance Indicators (KPIs) that reflect how well organisations are achieving their strategic objectives. The danger, though, is that a company can become so obsessed with improving its KPI measures that it stops fulfilling its true purpose.

The danger is that a company can become so obsessed with improving its KPI measures that it stops fulfilling its true purpose

In the UK's National Health Service, for example, patients have been left on trolleys in corridors for many hours so that they do not feature on waiting lists of those awaiting treatment in the hospital wards. Trains have been turned around three stops before the end of the line in order to meet their punctuality targets at the main line terminus. Police authorities have been found to be focusing on certain categories of crime that are easy to clear up while ignoring other, more serious, categories in order to boost their scores on the key indicators they are assessed on.

The key thing to remember about KPIs is that they should only be a guide as to whether you are going in the right general direction. They should not represent the end goals of the organisation.

The key thing to remember about KPIs is that they should only be a guide as to whether you are going in the right general direction

Are you unwittingly adopting someone else's success model?

If you adopt a set of KPI measures that consist of a particular consultancy's standard agree/disagree scale questions, you are, in effect, adopting *its* model of how *your* organisation should work. The danger is that this supplants the unique business model that your company may well have invested months developing and embedding. Maybe a small part of that will have to do with the kind of culture you want to create. However, it is unlikely that the way you have defined this will correspond particularly well to the kinds of attitudes that the consultancy is suggesting you measure using its standardised statements. Since the questions are standard questions, they have not in any way been customised to your own business strategy or your idea of how you define 'success'. Common sense and experience tells us that the kind of culture that makes an airline successful is different to a bank or a rail operator. They just have to focus on different things in order to succeed.

Do the questions mean different things in different organisations?

If you are going to include normative questions in a questionnaire, you should ensure that they are going to be interpreted in much the same way whichever organisation the question is being asked in. Good examples of where this is unlikely to be true are questions that refer to characteristics of the organisation that are unique to it, such as its vision, values, objectives and goals. These will be expressed quite differently in each organisation and will take quite different forms so will rarely be comparable from one organisation to the next. Statements such as *'I believe strongly in the goals and objectives of [Employer]'* or *'The mission of my company makes me feel my work is important'* will not be comparable across organisations.

Another flaw in these types of questions is that you often do not know what you are measuring and it varies by organisation. In some the scores will be driven by ignorance of what the items (e.g. goals) refer to, in others by confusion between different possible goals (e.g. corporate, divisional, team) in others by staff failing to understand what the question means. Consequently, the norms are rendered pretty well useless.

Another flaw in these types of question is that you often do not know what you are measuring

Similar issues arise with statements such as *'I am inspired by the person leading this organisation'.* Although well intentioned as a measure of the ability of the top management to inspire and motivate their staff, it is poor as a normative question for a number of reasons. Some cultures have a clearly defined 'leader' - Richard Branson at Virgin, for example. Many do not and, indeed, it is often the policy to play down the role of any one top person and perhaps to play up the role of local managers. Moreover, in organisations consisting of many divisions or subsidiaries, there will be different ideas of who the 'person leading the organisation' is since it depends which organisation one is talking about. In many cases, staff will not actually know the name of, say, the Chief Executive, since they have absolutely no dealings with them, and have no need to. Even if, as Best Companies do, you name the person who should be regarded as 'leading the organisation', it begs the question how far it is fair to compare a leader defined in one way in one organisation and in another way in a different organisation. And if inspiration, rather than the one leader, is the issue, then why focus on one inspiring leader but not other leaders, perhaps at a divisional or departmental level, who may be equally or more inspiring?

In this context, one should be cautious about drawing conclusions from the fact that your company's score is higher or lower than the 'norm'.

Are your composite norms being corrupted?

Some consultancies' 'norms' are in fact made up by calculating the average scores (e.g. percent agreeing with the statements) of a number of their standard statements. Towers Perrin/ISR does this in compiling its 'indices' for 'employee engagement' and 'customer focus', for example. Best Companies does this to create 'factor scores' for its eight factors that are used to calculate 'The Sunday Times Best 100 Companies to Work For' listing.

Here, if there are any statements that do not really fit your organisation, the whole index is corrupted. For the reasons given above, the Best Companies' statement, *'I am inspired by the person leading this organisation'*, may fit uneasily in many businesses, even if the 'leader' is named, and yet it feeds in to its 'leadership factor', which in turn determines the scores and rank positions of companies in the widely publicised Sunday Times listing.

Does the consultancy's ideal attitudinal profile really suit your business?

Underlying the consultancy's package of questions is a major assumption - that there is an ideal profile of attitude scores to which every company should aspire. While this may be true on the more general questions that measure overall staff morale or job satisfaction, it is unlikely to be true of questions relating to more specific aspects of the culture.

Underlying the consultant's package of questions is the major assumption that there is an ideal profile of attitude scores to which every company should aspire

The case for a job satisfaction measure

Thus, the more general kind of normative questions are likely to be the most useful and can be used as KPIs. Many companies use some kind of employer or job satisfaction question. It is notable, for example, that the one question that Gallup includes in its survey alongside its 12 ('Q12') agree/disagree scale statements, asks staff to rate their employer as 'a place to work' using a five-point satisfaction scale. Some, like Watson Wyatt, claim that this is not what employee surveys should be doing nowadays. In its view, the focus should be on 'commitment and engagement…because this is what drives performance'. I disagree. I believe it is critical to understand employee satisfaction and to have an overall measure of it. However, I also believe it should not be the only overall measure.

Recommendation and advocacy

One popular agree/disagree scale statement, that is sometimes used as a KPI, measures employees' propensity to recommend their employer as a place to work. Towers Perrin/ISR uses the statement *'I would recommend [Employer] as a good place to work'.* Best Companies' statement is *'I would strongly recommend working for this organisation to others'.* Other consultancies have their own variations.

The idea of 'recommendation' is a powerful one. If someone is willing to recommend their employer to others, one can assume that it must be doing a lot of things right. However, I believe the agree/disagree scale formulation of this question can be improved upon. One problem with it is that many people may be very committed to their employer and motivated by their job, but also recognise that it is not the sort of job that everyone, or even most people, would want to do or necessarily the sort of place many, or even most, people would want to work in. It therefore seems to me that a better core concept was that of 'speaking highly about' rather than 'recommending'.

It also seems to me that, just as employees can enhance their employer's reputation and the overall equity of its brand by talking it up, they can also damage the reputation and undermine its brand equity by talking it down. Disagreement with the scale statements does not capture this.

Just as employees can enhance their employer's reputation by talking it up, they can also damage its reputation by talking it down

Some years ago, I therefore devised a question designed to address these issues and also to distinguish between those who were passionately enthusiastic about the organisation to the point that they would take any opportunity to promote it, from those who were positive, but less overtly committed.

The question I came up with was this:

> ***Q Which of these phrases best describes the way you would speak to people outside of [Employer] about [Employer] as an employer[4]***
>
> *I would **speak highly** of [Employer] **without being asked***
>
> *I would **speak highly** of [Employer] if **I were asked***
>
> *I would be **neutral** towards [Employer] **if I were asked***
>
> *I would be **critical of** [Employer] **without being asked***
>
> *I would be **critical** of [Employer] if **I am asked***

(Since Rensis Likert had a type of scale named after him, perhaps this type of scale should be called the 'Hutton Scale'!)

Relationship Hierarchy Model

The question was used to measure the top two levels of a model I devised in the mid-1990s to illustrate how organisations grow by building relationships with their stakeholders. It was called the Relationship Hierarchy Model (or 'Hutton Hierarchy'!). The idea is that all relationships grow by moving through a series of levels: Awareness, Trust, Transaction, Satisfaction, Commitment and Advocacy. The model can apply to any of an organisation's stakeholder groups – customers, investors, local communities, the media, and, of course, employees.

In the case of employees, the 'Awareness', 'Trust' and 'Transaction' levels relate to the employee becoming aware of the company, having a sufficiently positive image of it to apply for a job there, and then entering into an employment contract with it. 'Satisfaction' is to do with their expectations from the employment being met or surpassed. 'Commitment' is about doing things that suggest a long-term commitment. 'Advocacy' is about being so absolutely committed, energised, enthralled and inspired by the organisation that they will tell anyone who is willing to listen just what a wonderful organisation it is!

If you manage to drive everyone up to that level, it is likely they will be doing most of the things you want them to do to ensure the organisation succeeds. There is likely to be high commitment, high productivity, good teamwork, great enthusiasm. Staff turnover will be low; indeed, the organisation will develop a reputation as *the* place to work. Advocacy and commitment will also feed back into the system generating more awareness, and trust in the employment market and greater job satisfaction internally.

Relationship Hierarchy Model

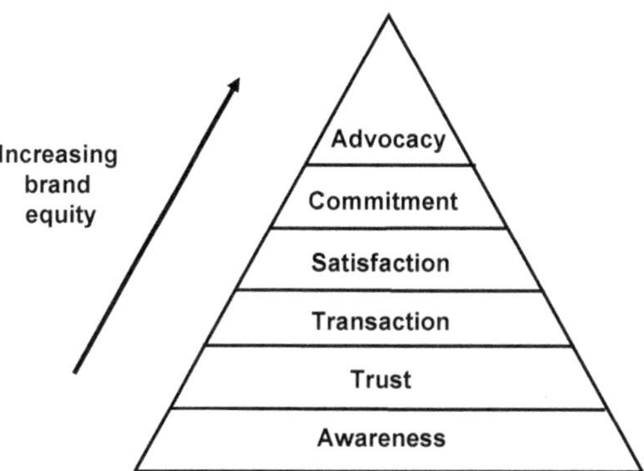

Of course, the same system can work the other way round. Negative advocacy undermines these levels and can cause the business to slow down or even go into reverse.

It also seemed to me that business success will not just be reflected in employees' propensity to talk highly about their employer as a place to work, but also to talk highly about what it does - its products or services. I therefore developed another question along the lines of:

> *Q Which of these phrases best describes the way you would speak to people outside of [Employer] about the products/services provided by [Employer].*

The same scale works for both versions. You might think that you would get similar results for each. In fact, generally you do not.

These questions could be seen to be measuring the strength of two critical brands of the organisation among its employees – its employer brand and its product or service brand. There is a third brand that could also be measured using the same scale. That is what I would call the 'corporate citizen brand'.[5] People are expecting more and more from major companies in terms of how they behave as 'corporate citizens' – socially, economically and environmentally. This area is currently rarely explored much in employee surveys, though I can see it gaining in importance especially as more companies place corporate responsibility and sustainability at the core of their corporate values.

The need to understand what is driving key measures

Your key measures may alert you to the fact that you have issues that need to be addressed, but rarely do they tell you what these issues are. A big part of the rest of the questionnaire should be about finding out what these are.

You can get some clues to this by cross-tabulating key questions by other questions in the questionnaire, but, in truth, that is normally a fairly blunt instrument.

Some consultancies will apply multivariate analysis to try to identify the 'key drivers' of their KPIs. However, as we discuss in the next section, this can generate quite misleading results and potentially steer you in the wrong direction.

Your key measures may alert you to the fact that you have issues that need to be addressed, but rarely do they tell you what these issues are

Questions designed to explore different facets of the business, such as internal communications, line management and performance barriers, can shed a lot of light on what is going wrong. However, if you want the best steer on what is driving a particular indicator, the best approach is often to simply ask a straight open-ended question immediately after the indicator question. Getting people to explain in their own words why they rated the company poorly is far more likely to point you towards the real causes than detailed analyses using questions that were not specifically designed to explain that particular question in the first place.

Many consultancies shy away from asking such 'open-ended' questions. Compared with pre-coded questions, they are time-consuming to collate and analyse, can be messy to interpret and can end up telling a rather different story than the one that emerges from standardised agree/disagree scale statements! Because, every response to every open-ended question needs to be read, collated and analysed, they can only be used sparingly. However, if the questions are well crafted, they are the ones that will best reflect the genuine voice of your staff, which ultimately is what you should be trying to capture through your employee survey.

The myths of multivariate analyses

Multivariate analyses look at the relationships between several variables in the questionnaire. Each question, or in the case of agree/disagree scales, each statement, is a separate variable. All respondents will answer the questionnaire in their own way producing a dataset with all the answers to all the questions from all the respondents.

Raw survey data in Excel format might look like this:

	A	B	C	D	E	F	G	H	I	J	K	L	M	N	O	P	Q	R	S
1	Cntry	ID	Pnt	Vers	Q1	Q2	Q3	Q4	Q5	Q6	Q7	Q8	Q9	Q10	Q11	Q12	Q14	Q15	Q16
2	1	1	1	1	1	4	4	4	2	9	3	1	3	9	5	5	2	1	3
3	1	2	1	1	6	2	2	2	4	2	2	3	2	3	3	3	1	1	2
4	1	3	1	1	2	4	9	3	2	3	3	1	2	9	5	5	1	1	2
5	1	4	1	1	1	2	3	2	2	2	3	1	2	3	5	5	1	2	2
6	1	5	1	1	1	2	1	2	2	2	2	3	2	9	5	5	1	1	3
7	1	6	1	1	1	3	2	2	2	2	2	3	2	9	5	5	1	1	2
8	1	7	1	1	1	2	4	2	2	3	3	1	3	9	5	3	1	2	2
9	1	8	1	1	1	1	1	2	2	2	1	3	2	4	5	5	1	1	4
10	1	9	1	1	1	3	4	1	4	3	2	1	3	3	5	3	2	1	3

Most multivariate analyses are designed to look at how far one variable moves up or down as other variables move up or down. In other words, do people who agree with statement A also tend to agree with statement B or C and so on.

Different kinds of analyses are then used to explore these relationships in different ways. Three of the most popular analyses applied by researchers to datasets based on agree/disagree statements are **correlation analysis**, **regression analysis** and **factor analysis**.

To undertake each of these, you basically need a set of questions that are all in the same format – like a five-point or seven-point scale. You then allocate a score to each point of the scale such as '1' for *disagree strongly*, '2' for *tend to disagree* up to '5' for *agree strongly*. Thus, a verbal scale is converted into a numerical scale. Alternatively, you may formulate the question to elicit the scores in the first place. Thus, you may ask respondents '*If '1' means strongly disagree and '5' means strongly agree, please indicated how far you agree or disagree with each of the following statements*'. Options then are 1, 2, 3, 4 and 5. It amounts to the same thing.

Having got your numerical scale you can then use **correlation analysis** to see how far different statements correlate with one another. In other words, how far do the scores given for different statements tend to go up and down together? Without going into the statistical detail, you can calculate a correlation coefficient that reflects this. A correlation coefficient of '+1' means the two variables are perfectly correlated so everyone who agrees strongly with statement A also agrees strongly with statement B; everyone who tends to agree with statement A also tends to agree with statement B and so on. A coefficient of '-1' means the opposite – everyone who strongly agrees with statement A strongly *dis*agrees with statement B and so on. A correlation coefficient of '0' means that there is no direct relationship between the answers on the two questions.

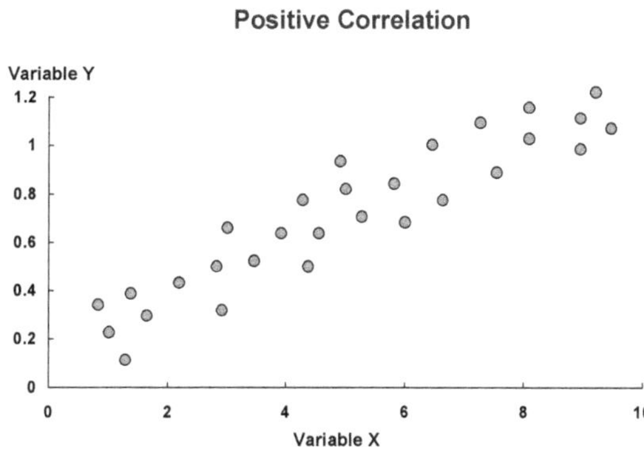

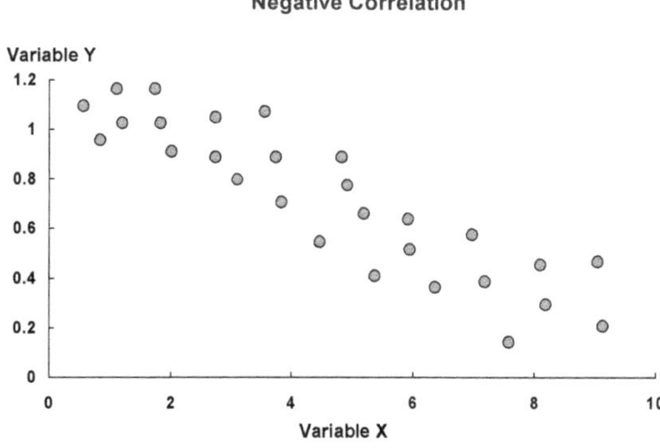

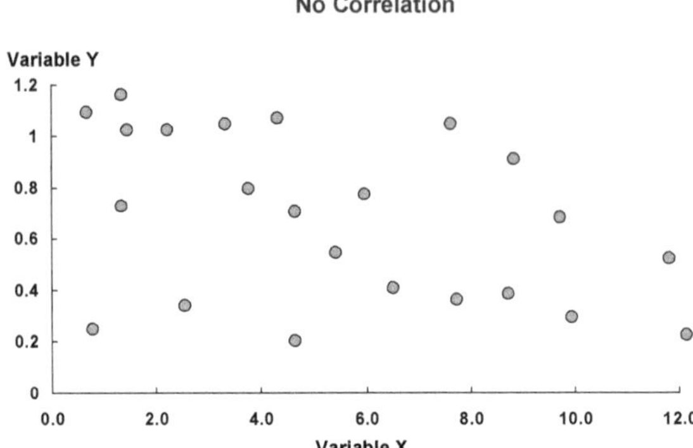

Correlation analysis (as well as regression analysis), played a key part in the development of the 12 statements that form the basis of the Gallup 'Q12' survey that I explore in more detail later. As well as using variables that were included in its surveys, it also used a series of variables that were completely independent of the survey. The ones it used were customer satisfaction, productivity, profitability and staff turnover. It was looking for the statements that appeared to be positively correlated with these variables.

Correlation analysis is also often used where you have a large number of statements and you believe that some of them may actually mean pretty much the same thing to respondents. By running a correlation analysis, you can identify those that correlate very highly i.e. respondents who agree with one also generally agree with the other. You might then decide to eliminate one of them from any further multivariate analysis and exclude it from future versions of your questionnaire.

Regression analysis is like correlation analysis, but is used to explore how far one 'dependent' variable appears to move up and down as another 'independent variable' moves up and down. Thus, the idea is that one variable's movements depend on the movement of another variable. The analysis will tell you how much of the variability of the dependent variable appears to be accounted for by the independent variable.

A variation of regression analysis is **multiple regression analysis.** The idea here is that you have one dependent variable and several independent variables. The way it works is that it first looks across the dataset to find the variable that records the highest level of variation with the dependent variable i.e. it accounts for more of the variation in that variable than any other variable in the dataset. It then looks for the variable that accounts for more of the remaining variability than any other remaining variable. The process continues until additional independent variables appear to account for a relatively small amount of the remaining variability of the dependent variable.

Multiple regression is sometimes used in employee surveys to identify what variables might be deemed most important to focus on to bring about desirable change in what the dependent variable is measuring (e.g. job satisfaction).

As we have seen, one of the real problems of surveys that consist of dozens, or even hundreds, of agree/disagree statements is that you just have no idea which are the most important ones to focus on. The agree/disagree format is not conducive to asking people which statements are the most or least important ones; it is just not a sensible thing to ask. Some consultants attempt to address this issue by using multiple regression analysis. First, they identify a dependent variable. This might be one of the attitude statements. Alternatively, questionnaires that are predominantly made up of agree/disagree statements, often have a few other types of question such as a five-point job satisfaction scale (ranging from *'very satisfied with your job'* to *'very dissatisfied'*). One of these would then be defined as the 'dependent variable'. The (other) agree/disagree statements are then used to find the 'key drivers' of that dependent variable. The argument is that if you know which variables appear to be 'driving' job satisfaction (say), then these are the ones to which you should pay most attention.

The approach also appears to address another issue with agree/disagree statement batteries; that of trying to make them join up to tell a coherent story. For some consultants there is something appealing about having a statistical solution to such a problem. It has the air of scientific objectivity, independence and robustness that few clients are likely to question.

Sadly, though, although this might initially sound a sensible and plausible approach, there are major problems associated with multiple regression analysis used in this way that can render the outcomes quite worthless.

There are major problems associated with multiple regression analysis that can render the outcomes quite worthless

The first thing to remember is that, if the intention is to use multiple regression analysis in the final stages of the research, you have to ensure the necessary variables are built into the questionnaire at the outset. They rarely are; moreover, there is a strong case for saying they never can be anyway. If staff are dissatisfied with their job, for example, there are scores of reasons why this may be the case. It is unlikely that all of them will be included in the attitude statements which you are using to find the 'drivers' of satisfaction or dissatisfaction, because the questionnaire was almost certainly not designed with that in mind in the first place.

That aside, because the agree/disagree scale only measures attitudes/opinions (and sometimes beliefs) anything that is not one of these cannot be derived from the analysis and defined as a 'driver' of job satisfaction. I have a real problem with the kind of model that says that one set of attitudes is driven by another set of attitudes. It is far more likely that employees' attitudes are driven by such things as the behaviours of their line managers, the climate of communication, the recognition and reward they receive and the support they get in doing their job. These may well be reflected in the attitudes they express, but that is not the same as saying that these attitudes are driving their overall job satisfaction.

I have a real problem with the kind of model that says that one set of attitudes is driven by another set of attitudes

Another issue relates to the nature of multiple regression. What researchers often fail to appreciate is that it works by first finding the variable that explains the most variation in the dependent variable; it then finds the variable that explains the *next* most amount of variation *after* the variation explained by the first variable has been taken out. What this means in practice is that a variable that is actually very important but that happens to correlate even just moderately highly with the first variable, is quite likely not even to feature as a 'key driver'.

Supporters of this approach will argue that they would first conduct correlation analysis and exclude one of any pairs of variables that correlate very highly together so that you are left with statements that appear to be measuring different things. There should then not be much overlap in the variability explained by each of the key variables. However, this has two innate problems. The first is, where do you draw the line? If the line is, say, a correlation coefficient of 0.75, why do you exclude a variable with a correlation coefficient of 0.76 but not one of 0.74? In other words, what is kept in and what is left out is a very grey area. The second is that where you have a very positive culture, you are likely to get very high scores on lots of things. It is then generally quite difficult to identify variables that correlate particularly highly with the dependent variable and thereby stand out as 'drivers'.

Finally, and related to the issue just described, statistically multiple regression assumes that all the variables being analyzed are independent of one another. In surveys like this, people are using the questionnaire to express their feelings about their experience of the organisation they work for and their own values. Consequently, many of the variables are generally not independent, but *inter*dependent. What you are often measuring is issues and feelings about different facets of the business that relate together in respondents' minds.

My concern with multiple regression is not confined to questionnaires that consist almost solely of agree/disagree statements. In surveys using a more varied mix of questions I have seen the 'key driver' analysis demonstrating one set of priorities for the business and more conventional analysis throwing up a completely different, and conflicting, set of priorities, without any explanation from the researchers as to why this should be! There was no doubt in my mind that the 'key driver' analysis was wrong and that the client would have been severely mistaken if they had made decisions based on that analysis.

Thus, for these reasons, multiple regression analysis provides an inadequate answer to the question of how to identify the issues to focus on. Far better than using multiple regression to find the 'key drivers' of satisfaction or, more usefully, dissatisfaction, is simply to ask a suitably crafted open-ended question!

I have seen 'key driver' analysis demonstrating one set of priorities and more a conventional analysis throwing up completely different, and conflicting, priorities

Factor analysis is another technique that is occasionally used in employee surveys. Best Companies used it to develop its 'Best Companies Factor Model of Workplace Engagement'.[6] Gallup also used it to reduce the number of statements with which it worked and to identify items that measured 'individual commitment'. Other consultancies that start out with lots of standard, or bespoke, agree/disagree statements occasionally use it (or a similar technique called principal component analysis) to help reduce their datasets to something more manageable.

Factor analysis is used to detect underlying structures in the data. For example, if you have asked a lot of people how strongly they agree or disagree with a large number of statements, there will be people who agree with some statements who also have a strong propensity to agree with other statements. The correlations of answers across the data set will suggest that there are certain themes that run through people's perceptions that are reflected in the way they respond to different groups of statements. Factor analysis sets out to determine what these 'themes' are. It does this by creating a series of virtual variables that account for as much of the variability of the data as possible, 'explaining' this variability in terms of the existence of these factors. Normally, the researchers will try various factor solutions to find the optimum number of factors that will explain the most variation of responses across the dataset without any factor explaining such a small amount of variation that its inclusion adds little of value. The factors can overlap in the sense that two factors can explain the variability of some of the same items (statements) and can correlate to some degree with one another. (In this respect, factor analysis is different from principal component analysis.)

Sometimes the factors are given labels that reflect the meaning of the variables whose variability they most 'explain'. As we see later, Best Companies identified eight factors that explained the most variability across its dataset of around 134 statements. The factor it labelled 'My Team', for example, particularly explained the variability of their statements that related to encouraging a team spirit, feeling part of the organisation, having fun and belonging.

The approach is not used widely in employee research for a number of reasons. First, not many employee researchers understand it! Second, to gain any benefit from it, you need to spend a considerable amount of time in developing appropriate items (statements) in order to undertake the analysis. Third, it is likely to require nearly all your questionnaire be devoted to collecting the data for this analysis rather than for other purposes. Finally, it is questionable how beneficial the end analysis actually is!

Although there are debates about how factor analysis should be applied and interpreted, it comes out of a school of thought that believes that individual statements used in attitude surveys taken in isolation provide a very partial and misleading view of how people think and feel about a particular issue. To get at this, you need to ask about a number of carefully constructed statements then apply a factor analysis to identify the underlying 'factor', 'construct' or 'core attitude' that the individual statements are measuring.

It is without doubt true that any individual item will give only a partial view. It is also true that people use attitude statements as a way of expressing views, e.g. grievances, which may have little directly to do with the explicit focus of the statement. Indeed, this is one of the key criticisms of the agree/disagree technique that I highlight in this book. One statement may be symptomatic of a large number of potential underlying issues that the person is responding to, while one underlying issue might be expressed in a large number of different agree/disagree measures, as the following chart illustrates.

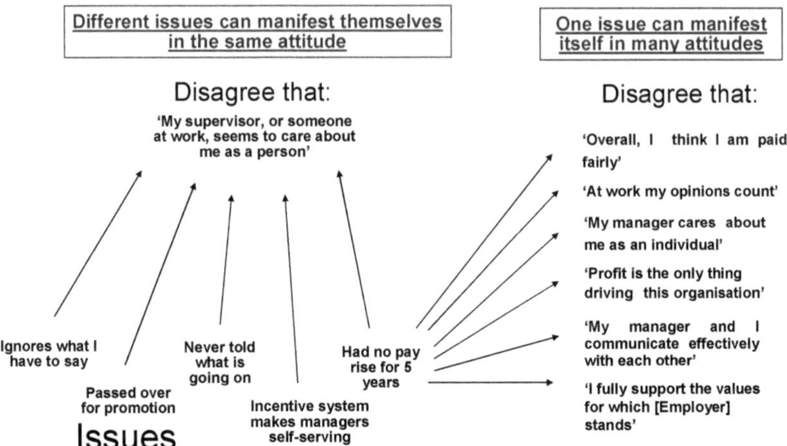

The 'solution' that factor analysis proposes is to use the correlations between the different statement measures to find the underlying factor or factors that account best for the variability of the data. These factors are believed to encapsulate the essence of what the different statements are measuring, and are assumed to exist irrespective of whether or not the research is done to establish their existence.

I have a number of issues with this way of thinking. From a theoretical point of view, I find the idea that there is one underlying factor/construct/core attitude, or a small number of them that the individual statements measure, questionable. Whatever the theory says, it seems to me that the factor really only exists as a result of the analysis. It is inextricably linked to the statements that are used to derive it. In the world of employee surveys, there is no end to the number of statements that can be formulated to express the way people feel about different aspects of their work experience. If a different set of statements is used in the analysis, a different set of factors will emerge. If there are, as proponents of factor analysis might suggest, a core and implicitly pretty stable set of factors, then each set of analyses using different statements will come up with a pretty fuzzy set of definitions of what they are, which I am not sure is that helpful.

That aside, as the example above illustrates, attitudes in the workplace are often driven by employees' experiences. Here, someone who has had no pay rise for five years, for example, may be pretty aggrieved and express this in a number of different attitude statements, none of which point directly to that as the primary cause. Nonetheless, in as far as it is the primary cause, it is not something that will be revealed through factor analysis.

I also have a problem with those who undertake this kind of analysis on questions asked across scores, if not hundreds, of organisations then proclaim they have discovered some kind of universal 'factors' that apply to all organisations. Different companies have different cultures as well as different visions, missions, strategies and objectives; so why should exactly the same set of statements be appropriate for an airline as a local council? And why should the factor solutions be the same in each organisation? Statistically this is unlikely, but where it does appear to be the case, it seems to me it is most likely due to the similarity of subject matter – statements relating to management style are more likely to correlate with other statements about management style than with statements about, pay and benefits, for example.

For consultancies that have let the process of questionnaire development get out of hand, such that they end up with hundreds of statements and no clear picture of what is going on, a factor analysis (or principal component analysis) can seem like a welcome gleam of hope. What joy to be able to reduce it all to, say, seven or eight factors rather than 237 statements!

Although the factors may help you to make sense of the kinds of patterns that appear to lie beneath the surface of your data, they are actually rarely very useful

Alas, they are likely to be disappointed. Although the factors/components may help you to make sense of the kinds of patterns that appear to lie beneath the surface of your data, in themselves they are actually rarely very useful. OK, you can take the factors as variables, like individual statements and see how scores on them vary by different groups of employees. However, because in reality they are derived from lots of different variables (responses to statements) they are actually very complex instruments and difficult to interpret.

It is also too sweeping a view to dismiss the usefulness of individual items. Many single item agree/disagree statements are very useful in employee surveys especially where they are designed to test hypotheses about what people believe or think. Factor analysis belongs to an altogether more theoretical world where understanding the ultimate nature of perceptions may be a priority, but in management this is generally not the case.

Use of factor analysis can make more sense in marketing research where you are trying to understand consumer markets that you are some way removed from, particularly those linked closely to changing tastes and fashion. Successful marketing here depends on identifying, often quite subtle, emotional needs and anxieties that the products can be positioned to address – washing powders are about being a conscientious and caring mother, deodorants are about male/female attraction, diamonds are about love and commitment and so on. Typically, it will involve extensive qualitative research in the form of focus groups to understand why consumers buy different brands in the product category and the attitudes associated with their brand preferences. These attitudes will be converted into agree/disagree statements and presented to a large sample of consumers – certainly several hundred and probably over a thousand - in the target audience. The responses will be converted into scores and used to generate factors that summarise the meaning of a very wide range of attitudes. For brand development purposes, these factors can point to different market segments. Factors derived from consumer attitudes to breakfast cereals, for example, might discover one factor being about ensuring your children have the right vitamins and a nutritious start to the day; another about the healthy option for older people, avoiding excessive sugar, fat and salt whereas another may focus on price and value for money and so on. Used in this way, it is as much as anything a device to help marketers and the creatives in advertising agencies to deliver the right message, tone, feel and style of the brand through their marketing communications.

The need to segment the target population in order to engage them with different, essentially emotional, messages does not exist in the same way for the employer brand. While you clearly want to engage your staff with what the organisation is about and where it is trying to go, you are more likely to want to have one consistent set of messages and feel for the organisation than subtly different messages for different parts of the organisation. The exception might be where you have quite different businesses within an overall group of companies where it makes sense to nurture different cultures.

However, it is unlikely that undertaking a major staff survey with scores of attitude statements followed by a factor analysis will help a great deal. A far more qualitative research exercise involving workshops focusing on different aspects of the business and the work experience, perhaps followed by a simple testing of the various propositions that emerge, is likely to be far more useful.

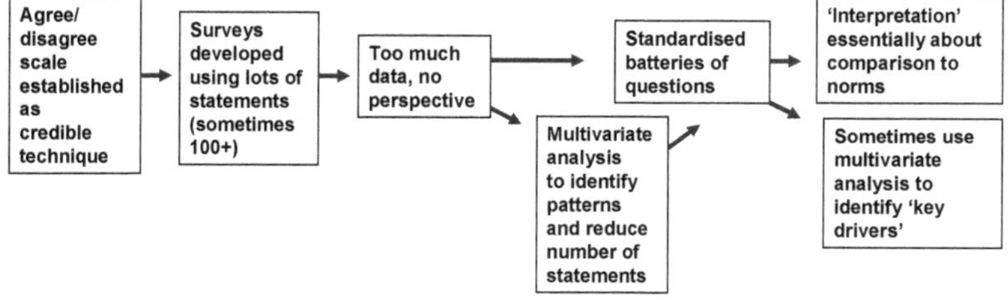

A tale of two companies

In exploring the use made of multivariate analysis using agree/disagree scale data, two companies in particular have been cited as examples: Gallup and Best Companies. These two companies have applied these techniques far more extensively than other employee research consultancies. From this, they have derived their own unique sets of questions that each has put at the core of their employee research offerings.

They have also made extraordinary claims about the value and significance of these questions. But are they justified in making these claims? Do the agree/disagree statements they present really possess the power to transform business performance that their literature implies that they do? And do the conclusions they draw really follow from the statistical analyses that they applied?

Gallup and its 'Q12' questions

History and business model

The name 'Gallup' is synonymous with opinion measurement. George Gallup was the founding father of modern market research. He was born in Iowa in 1901, gained a doctorate degree at the University of Iowa, taught at various US Universities and started applying survey research techniques in a variety of fields. In 1932, he joined the advertising agency, Young and Rubicam, heading up its marketing and copy research departments. While there, he began his work in the field of public opinion and election forecasting.

In 1935, he set up the American Institute of Public Opinion, which later became the Gallup Organisation. It was here that his surveys created a breakthrough that was to lay the foundations for public opinion polling throughout the world. In 1936, he predicted that Franklin Roosevelt would win that year's US presidential election while the well-respected Literary Digest predicted a landslide for Alfred Langdon. The Literary Digest mailed hundreds of thousands of people whose names were in telephone or car ownership directories, a relatively small proportion of the population in those days, and heavily skewed to more affluent electors. Gallup, by contrast, had followed sound survey principles to ensure that its sample was representative of the US electorate. Its final poll findings closely reflected the ultimate vote of the electorate.

Over the next two decades, businesses bearing the Gallup name sprang up across the globe. In 1958, they were brought together under the umbrella of The Gallup Organisation.

Although Gallup was most widely known for its public opinion polls covering voting intention and an extraordinary wide range of social and political topics, its main revenues came from its market research activities. It also conducted employee attitude surveys. By the time George Gallup died in 1984, the Gallup Organisation was a truly international brand with a reputation for independence, objectivity and professionalism in all it research activities.

In 1988, it was acquired by Selection Research Incorporated (SRI) in Lincoln, Nebraska. SRI's roots were in recruitment consulting, conducting structured psychological interviews to identify the talents of individuals who 'fit' a designated position or role in an organisation.

It seems to me that SRI was a far more commercially minded organisation than Gallup and recognised that the Gallup brand was punching vastly below its full commercial potential. Over the next decade, it increased Gallup's business volume tenfold and expanded into twenty countries. It did this by repositioning Gallup as a consultancy rather than a research agency and focusing particularly on major, often international, on-going customer satisfaction tracking surveys and employee attitude surveys using its standardised 'Q12' list of 12 questions.

If the main objective was to generate huge amounts of profit, the new business model was far more likely to be successful. George Gallup truly believed in research as a means of learning and reporting "the will of the people" and as an important part of the democratic process. As such, generating massive growth and high profits were probably not very high on his agenda. By contrast, they were clearly very high on SRI's agenda. Most of Gallup's business would have been relatively small-scale social and political polls and market and employee research studies. The vast majority of these would have generated far less than $15,000 revenue each. By contrast, the revenues from well-crafted customer satisfaction and employee research propositions, pitched at top management, can be enormous. Large-scale customer satisfaction surveys involving lots of interviews on a rolling programme, that integrate into the management and reward systems, can create very substantial revenues streams while being run as fairly low-cost, process-driven operations.

The proposition for the employee research was somewhat different. SRI could have opted for the traditional, pragmatic, Gallup approach; a mixture of standardised questions developed over a number of years and bespoke questions developed to meet individual client needs. However, clients would not pay a premium for what they would see as a traditional research approach. It could have settled on a standard set of questions for every survey thereby cutting out the costs involved in customising surveys and charging a premium for access to its exclusive normative database. However, it would need to justify why its questions were any more appropriate than any other consultancy that was offering a standard set of questions.

What it appears to have ended up doing was developing a proposition that reflected its roots in psychological profiling, but that was presented as being grounded in the hundreds of surveys conducted by Gallup over the previous 25 years.

The challenge it faced was how to leverage Gallup's assets – its solid reputation for objective, robust research, plus 25 years of employee survey data – together with its own assets – its expertise in psychological profiling and its core belief that recruiting and retaining the right people is the key to achieving outstanding performance. The solution it hit on was to analyse the Gallup employee survey data to find a handful of key questions that 'measure the core elements needed to attract, focus and keep the most talented employees'[7]. What companies and managers are looking for, so it claims, is 'a simple and accurate measuring stick that can tell them how well one company or one manager is doing compared with others in terms of finding and keeping talented people. Without that measuring stick many companies and many managers know they may find themselves high and dry'[8].

If it could prove that, irrespective of the organisation, the same handful of questions appeared to correlate with better business performance, then it could claim a major advantage over the competition. It is, in fact, an extremely difficult, some might say impossible, thing to prove convincingly. However, that is what it set out to do.

The so-called 'Q12' questions were the product of a very extensive exercise involving a great deal of statistical analysis and subjective judgement. The result has been a proposition quite unlike any other consultancy. It asks just 12 standard agree/disagree scale questions (statements) plus a five-point scale measuring satisfaction with the organisation as a place to work. The selling point is that these are the key measures you have to get right to ensure your commercial indicators are going in the right direction. The vast bulk of its revenue comes neither from questionnaire design – there is none – nor from collecting the data – most of this cost is borne by the client – but in charging for normative comparisons and providing expertise in interpreting what the responses mean. Often the latter involves its consultants facilitating workshops to try to work through what the results mean for different parts of the business.

But how robust is the analysis? Were the correlations as conclusive as the claims for the questions would imply? Can one really draw conclusions about *any* organisation based on questions that were derived from analysing data from surveys conducted across a small number of completely different organisations? Is it right to ask questions only about attitudes that (it is claimed) relate to the attraction and retention of highly motivated people rather than a whole host of other factors that determine organisational performance? Is it at all clear what the answers to the questions mean for any particular organisation? Does the evidence support Gallup's assertion that it has discovered the questions that 'capture the *most* information and the most *important* information' about the strength of your workplace.[9]

Let us begin by exploring how Gallup's 'Q12' questions were derived.

How Gallup derived its 'Q12' questions

In their book, 'First Break All the Rules', published in 1999, Marcus Buckingham and Curt Coffman, set out to explain why and how they came up with Gallup's 12 ('Q12') questions. These were the questions that, they suggest, would define the 'core elements' that would create 'the kind of workplace that can attract, focus and keep the most talented employees'. [10]

The process of deriving these final 12 questions evolved through a number of phases. First, they tell us, all the questions Gallup had asked across numerous organisations over 25 years, were distilled down to a much smaller number. Then regression analysis was used to see which of these appeared to drive a number of 'dependent' variables. Then correlation analysis was used to demonstrate that higher scores on these questions (or statements) correlated with higher scores on a range of business performance measures, specifically customer satisfaction/loyalty, profitability, productivity and employee turnover.

How the 'Q12' statements were derived

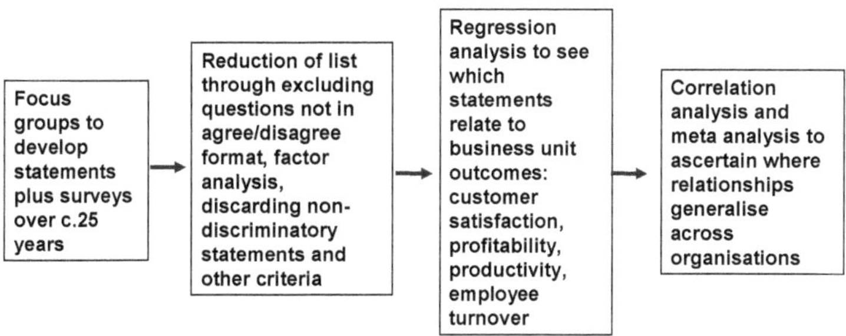

In more detail, the authors tell us that Gallup conducted focus groups and from these they developed 'lengthy surveys'. These were administered to 'over one million employees'. After each study, the authors claim, analyses were performed 'to identify the factors within the data', i.e. a factor analysis (see p62 to explain what this is). [11]

In reality, it seems highly implausible that such factor analysis was conducted after each study since many of the questions would have been unsuited to conducting such analysis. Nevertheless, according to the authors, five factors consistently emerged. These had to do with:

1. The work environment/procedures
2. Immediate supervisor
3. Team/co-workers
4. Overall company/senior management
5. Individual commitment/service intention

This analysis seems to have been used in two ways to home in on the final 'Q12' questions. First, it was used to identify statements that defined 'individual commitment' for its later analysis. Second, it was probably used as a device for reducing the list of statements by excluding those whose variability was not explained by these factors.

However, most of the exclusion of questions was more likely to have been done in a non-statistical way. Although Buckingham and Coffman's account of the methodology, implies that the '100 million' questions that they 'ran through their prism' to break out the most important questions, were all in the same format and that all the different survey datasets were subjected to the same rigorous analysis in order to find the ultimate gems, this was almost certainly not the case. For a start, it seems that only questions that conformed to the agree/disagree format were acceptable, which it likely to have excluded questions measuring behaviours, motivations and knowledge. At the very least, the questions needed to be in a scale format, otherwise they would not produce data that could be used in Gallup's regression analysis. Thus, any question using a list could not be included and neither could open-ended questions. Moreover, any questions developed to meet the bespoke needs of any particular client could not qualify.

It seems that only questions that conformed to the agree/disagree format were acceptable, which it likely to have excluded questions measuring behaviours, motivations and knowledge.

The authors also tell us that questions that generally seemed to get very high levels of people either agreeing or disagreeing strongly were also excluded as they would not discriminate between different kinds of respondent. In addition, questions that showed very high levels of correlation that suggested they meant pretty much the same thing to respondents resulted in one of them being excluded.[12]

The authors also explain how it was decided to exclude questions that were thought to be a 'shoo-in – like those dealing with pay and benefits'.

Gallup then performed various regression analyses (see p58 for explanation) on the data 'to identify some of the most powerful questions within the dataset'. These, one assumes, were the ones that showed the highest level of regression to (or correlation with) the dependent variables. The dependent variables it used for this analysis were:

> **Overall satisfaction with the organisation as a place to work** – the five-point scale question used alongside the 'Q12' questions.
>
> **The five best questions from the individual commitment factor** – presumably the statements that correlated most highly with the fifth factor found in the factor analysis. Although it is not explained why it chose factors exclusively from that one factor, it is probably to do with fact that their model of what drives performance requires staff that are both 'loyal and productive'.[13]
>
> **The performance outcomes of the business units** - measures of customer satisfaction/loyalty, profitability, productivity, and staff turnover.

Before selecting its final 12 questions, it then added a criterion that the questions had to be 'simple and easy to effect. They had to be "actionable" not emotional outcome questions like '*Overall how satisfied are you with your work environment?*' or '*Are you proud to be working for you company?*'.[14]

Gallup is somewhat protective of its 12 questions, or rather agree/disagree statements. It goes to great lengths to ensure no one reproduces them, even though they are listed on page 284 of Buckingham and Coffman's book. They all relate to the work place and the gist of each one is as follows:

1. *Knowing what is expected of you*
2. *Having the right materials and equipment to do your job*
3. *Having the opportunity at work to do what you do best*
4. *Receiving recognition for doing good work*
5. *Having someone who seems to care about you*
6. *Having someone who encourages your development*
7. *Feeling that your opinions count*

8. *A perception that the mission/purpose of your company makes you feel that your job is important*
9. *A perception that your fellow employees are committed to doing quality work*
10. *Having a best friend at work*
11. *Having had someone talk to you about your progress in the last six months*
12. *Having had opportunities to learn and grow in the last year*

Having identified these 'twelve most powerful questions', it then subjected them to 'rigorous confirmatory analyses'. The meta-analysis presented in the book was one such study. Meta-analysis aims, as best it can, to draw conclusions from across a large and complex dataset with inconsistent variables. In this case, it focused on looking at the correlations between the 'Q12' statements and the business outcome measures.

The analysis was conducted using 28 studies across twenty-four separate companies. To provide sufficient data points to undertake the analysis, the organisations were broken down by business unit. In that way, for any one organisation, you have the survey data – the average scores on each of the 12 statements - and business performance measures, for each business unit. In this case it was able to work with data from just over 2,500 business units.

The reason why this kind of analysis is rarely done and has probably never been done well, is that ideally you need a) lots of case studies b) longitudinal data, not just data covering one period or point in time and c) consistent types of measurement between organisations. This is pretty well impossible to achieve and did not apply to the Gallup analysis.

Although it split data across 2,528 business units, the information was still patchy. Of the 28 studies included in the analysis, the most it was able to include for any one business outcome variable, was 18. Profitability measures were only available for 14 of the businesses. Moreover, different companies produced different kinds of data for each of the variables. Indeed, in the case of the productivity variables, some of the 'measures' were actually managerial judgements as to which business units were most 'productive'.

The sample was also heavily skewed towards organisations that happened to have a reasonably large number of business units that could be compared. Thus, 59% of all the business units included in the analysis were from either retail or financial services organisations – i.e. ones with large branch networks.

The meta-analysis examined two hypotheses, that:

1. Employee perceptions of quality of management practices measured by the 13 core items (the 'Q12' statements plus one job satisfaction scale question) are related to business unit outcomes (i.e. units with higher scores on these items have, in general, more favourable business outcomes).

2. The validity of employee perceptions of quality of management practices measured by the 13 Core items generalises across the organisations studied.[15]

The two hypotheses were confirmed. However, it is questionable whether the confirmations mean that the question are an effective tool of management or support Gallup's assertion that Gallup the questions 'capture the *most* information and the most *important* information' about the strength of your workplace.[16]

Critique of the 'Q12'

It did seem to be an extraordinary proposition that you could now discard your more traditional, bespoke employee survey questionnaire and replace it with one that consisted of a standardised list of just 12 agree/disagree statements and one job satisfaction question. Yet this seemed to be what Gallup were suggesting. However, there are many grounds for being wary of this approach and the rationale behind it. These include the following.

The links are counter-intuitive

The authors note that all of the 'Q12' questions were linked to at least one of the four business outcomes – productivity, profitability, employee retention and customer satisfaction[17]. Some questions correlated with some outcomes, some with others, though it is difficult to fathom any underlying logic to the findings, especially as some of them seem counter intuitive. Staff turnover, for example, correlated with having the materials and equipment staff need for their job, but not with having someone at work encouraging their development or with a receiving recognition and praise. Customer satisfaction seemed to be related to having a best friend at work but not to their colleagues being committed to doing quality work or to their having the materials and equipment they need.

Wrongly implied causality

The fact that there is a statistical correlation between the 'Q12' statements and the business outcome measures, does not mean that the former drive the latter. Admittedly, the authors never say that they do, though it is strongly implied. One of the problems we have highlighted with attitude measurement in employee surveys is that you are often measuring the symptoms of what is happening

One problem with attitude measurement in employee surveys is that you are generally measuring the symptoms of what is happening in the business and rarely the deep-rooted causes. This is likely to be true of the 'Q12' questions.

in the business environment and rarely the deep-rooted causes. This is likely to be true of the Gallup questions.

There is a saying among statisticians that 'correlation does not equal causation'. Often if two variables correlate together, it is not that one drives the other but rather that another factor that is not included in the analysis is influencing both. If there is a direction of causation in this case, it seems most likely that it is not so much positive staff attitudes driving business performance, but business performance driving positive staff attitudes.

You can see how this could have worked with Gallup's meta-analysis. Most of this was undertaken on data from the branches of retailers and financial service organisations. Clearly, some branches will have performed better than others, for a whole variety of reasons that need have nothing to do with the staff at the branch. Location, for example; they may be in more affluent areas, or better placed for passing footfall in the High Street, or in areas where the competition is relatively weak.

Because these branches are more successful, the company is likely to invest more in them – e.g. more staff and higher calibre staff, better décor and facilities, etc. In successful, growing branches, it would be easier to attract staff and achieve higher levels of job satisfaction. There would be greater recognition for achievement, more opportunities to develop careers, and a greater feeling of the importance of their job. Customers would be more satisfied because they are given more, and better, facilities and staff are able to provide a wider range of products/services to a higher standard than in the less successful branches at the wrong end of the High Street. Thus, the greater success of those branches will be reflected, not only in the business outcome measures of customer satisfaction, profitability, productivity and staff turnover, but also in Gallup's 'Q12' attitude measures. However, it is not that the more positive staff attitudes have driven business performance but rather that the business performance has driven more positive staff attitudes. This interpretation has major implications for how, or even whether, you should respond to the research findings.

Questions are not unique nor necessarily the best for measuring the 'strength of the workplace'

It is possibly true, as the authors assert, that 'if you can create the kind of environment where employees answer positively to all 12 questions, then you will have built a great place to work'. However, that is almost certainly as true for a host of other questions that are asked by other consultancies. Moreover, the fact that the measures were derived from analyses of data across many different organisations does not necessarily make them better measures of 'the strength of the workplace' for any *particular* organisation. Every organisation is different and many will have characteristics that make them distinctively attractive places to work. They may, for example have a particularly inspiring vision or charismatic leader, but that will not be reflected in the 'Q12' statements.

Responses are largely in-actionable

If there is no causative link between the 'Q12' questions and business performance, one has to wonder what is the point of measuring these attitudes in the first place? They do not help you to understand how you can improve performance and they are not substitute measures for the business outcomes they are linked with. Even if you accept that they are good indicators that a company has 'arrived', that does not mean that these are the measures they need to tell them *how* to arrive. As we indicate above, they are likely to be symptoms of deeper-rooted issues that management needs to address. However, none of the Gallup questions identify what these issues are.

Although high scores on these questions might be an indication that the company has 'arrived', that does not mean that these are the measures management need to tell them how to arrive

Ironically, at one point the authors stress that they set the (sensible) criterion that the questions 'had to be "actionable" questions,[18] not emotional outcome questions like '*Overall how satisfied are you with your work environment?*' or '*Are you proud to be working for your company?*''. However, the questions they settled on do not seem to be much more actionable.

There is not much you can do about the fact that a large proportion of staff do not feel that at work they 'have a best friend' or 'know what is expected of them' since you do not know to what they are referring. All you have is a vague indication that you may have some kind of issues in these broad areas, but no understanding of what these issues are.

Similarly, knowing that a lot of staff do not feel the 'mission or purpose of their company makes them feel that what they do is important' is also problematical. The response suggests that there is an issue to be dealt with, but not what that issue is. Is it, for example, that staff know what the mission/purpose is, but it does not make them feel their work is important? Or is it that they have never come across the company's mission/purpose?

Whether someone feels they 'have a best friend at work' seems an odd issue to include and the action possibilities are far from clear, apart, perhaps, from running speed-dating sessions in the lunch break or having a 'bring a friend' recruitment drive!

Most of the statements do, though, relate to things that many other studies have demonstrated are important to staff. The problem with asking only those 12 statements, though, is that there is no further information to shed light on what you can do about any one of them. An open-ended question to follow up those who indicate that they do not have the materials or equipment they need, for example, would help to ascertain whether it is just a general failure of the IT system or different kinds of issues in different areas of the organisation. However, the 'Q12' surveys do not incorporate such questions.

The problem with asking only those 12 statements is that there is no further information to shed light on what you can do about any one of them

Do not distinguish 'motivators' and 'satisfiers'

Another criticism of the 'Q12' statements is that they fail to recognise a particularly powerful insight into how people are affected by their working environment. Frederick Hertzberg was a US clinical psychologist and later professor of management who was one of the most influential thinkers in his field. His book, 'The Motivation to Work', was published in 1959 and outlined his research-based finding that satisfaction and dissatisfaction arise from quite different factors. Dissatisfaction, he discovered, arises essentially from the absence of 'hygiene' factors. These include things like: the organisation's policies and administration, the kind of management staff receive, working conditions including the physical working environment, interpersonal relations, salary, and job security. Satisfaction, on the other hand, comes from the presence of a different set of factors that he termed 'motivators'. These include things such as achievement, recognition, interest in the job and growth and advancement.

In refining down the list of key questions, the authors imply that most hygiene factors were purposely excluded from consideration as key variables. They noted that:

> '...there are no questions in their 12 dealing with pay, benefits, senior management, or organisational structure. There were, initially but they disappeared during the analysis. This does not mean that they were not important. It simply means they are equally important to every employee, good, bad and mediocre'

This assertion flies in the face of the evidence from thousands of other studies that clearly show that factors such as 'pay and benefits' are not 'equally important to every employee'. Perhaps what they were really trying to say was that they were not 'motivational', which would be consistent with what Herzberg was saying. However, that does not explain why some of their final statements clearly related to hygiene factors such as having the right equipment for the job or a best friend at work.

Omits many critical questions

Moreover, there are many other aspects of the job and work environment that research has shown to be important, both hygiene and motivational factors, that are excluded from the 'Q12'. In part, this appears to be due to the fact that Gallup's 'model' of what drives business success is essentially driven by the idea that you need to 'attract and motivate the right people', rather than anything else. It also appears that Gallup only wanted a small number of key questions, which severely limits the scope of any survey. Moreover, being confined to the agree/disagree scale format meant that many important aspects could not be included in the most sensible way. The inevitable consequence, in my view, is that the most important questions that should be asked in an employee survey are not included in the 'Q12'.

Conclusion

In view of all this, there seems no substance in the claim that the 'Q12' questions 'capture the *most* information and the most *important* information' about the strength of your workplace.

A client's perspective?

You can imagine a conversation between someone from Gallup and one of its more enquiring clients.

Mr C: Before you present the research findings to our Board, the chairman has asked me to clarify a couple of points about your 'Q12' questions.

Mr G: Fine, go ahead.

Mr C: The first question is how do we interpret the results? For example, according to the survey, X percent agreed with the statement about 'my supervisor caring about me as a person'. How do we interpret that?

Mr G: Well, X percent is below the norm for companies like yours.

Mr C: Meaning?

Mr G: Meaning that the percent agreeing with that statement in your company is a bit below the score we get if we average all the percentages agreeing with that statement from all the companies that we have asked that question in.

Mr C: I see. So, not brilliant then?

Mr G: No. You should be aiming to improve on that.

Mr C: And how do we do that?

Mr G: What do you mean?

Mr C: Well, what does the research tell us about why so many of our staff believe that no one at work seems to care about them?

Mr G: Ah, well, there is nothing in the research that tells you *why* they feel that way.

Mr C: Oh?

Mr G: No, it was only designed to tell you what your employees feel on these critical questions. It was not designed to tell you how to improve on these measures!

Mr C: I see. And what makes them so 'critical' as questions?

Mr G: We undertook a major analysis on the questions that Gallup asked in its employee surveys over 25 years.

Mr C: And what did you achieve from this analysis?

Mr G: Well, we managed to boil down all the questions to just 12 that we believe are the simplest and most accurate way to measure the strength of a workplace.

Mr C: Just twelve, eh? So how did you derive these twelve questions?

Mr G: Well, in Gallup we used to conduct focus groups among our clients' employees to decide what questions to ask their staff.

Mr C: Sounds sensible.

Mr G: Then we realised that a lot of the same issues were coming up so we ended up asking a lot of the same questions in lots of different companies.

Mr C: I see.

Mr G: But we still had lots of different questions and we wondered if we could reduce it to a much smaller number.

Mr C: Like twelve!

Mr G: Exactly, like twelve.

Mr C: Can I clarify something?

Mr G: Go ahead.

Mr C: I notice that all your twelve questions measure attitudes and all use the same agree/disagree question format.

Mr G: That is correct.

Mr C: So does that mean that all the questions that Gallup asked over 25 years only measured attitudes and were all in the agree/disagree format?

Mr G: Oh no. It asked about lots of different kinds of things using lots of different formats.

Mr C: Oh, I see. So how come all the questions in your 'Q12' list are in this agree/disagree format and only measure attitudes? Does that mean that questions in a different format or that measured anything other than attitudes are not as good at measuring the 'strength of the workplace'?

Mr G: Not necessarily, no. We did consider these other questions but they did not fit our approach.

Mr C: Your approach?

Mr G: Yes, you see in order to find the most powerful questions we undertook regression analysis to see which questions appeared to correlate with a number of business performance measures such as profitability, productivity and staff turnover.

Mr C: I see.

Mr G: And to do this we needed questions in a format that would fit the analysis, like the five-point agree/disagree scale questions.

Mr C: I see, so any questions that consisted of a list, for example, where employees could express their preferences, clearly would not fit that format so would have been excluded.

Mr G: Yes, I suppose you are right.

Mr C: So, just to be clear, the criterion for questions being included in your analysis was that they should be in the agree/disagree format and all other questions that did not fit into that format were excluded even though they may have been highly relevant and important?

Mr G: Yes, I suppose that could have been true.

Mr C: I see. And, just to be clear again, the questions you included presumably they were all standard questions that you had used in lots of different companies?

Mr G: Yes, that is right.

Mr C: So, if Gallup had found that in a particular company, one particular aspect of the business was important to cover in its staff survey, but it had not come up in quite a number of other companies, then the questions developed to cover that aspect were not included in your analysis?

Mr G: Yes, you could say that. We only included standard questions that had been used across quite a number of different companies.

Mr C: And were any of the interviews that you included in your analysis conducted in our company?

Mr G: Oh no. These were conducted in companies all over the world, mostly over ten years ago.

Mr C: I see. So the questions we have just asked in our staff survey were never developed specifically for *our* business?

Mr G: I suppose you could say that.

Mr C: OK. So please explain how we ended up with these particular questions.

Mr G: Well, first we took the data from lots of different surveys and undertook what we call 'correlation analysis'. Often questions will correlate so closely together that they are probably measuring the same thing so we can drop some of them. Also, we decided to exclude questions where we generally found high levels of agreement or disagreement, as they would not differentiate between different groups of employees very well.

Mr G: I see.

Mr G: Then we undertook the regression analysis.

Mr C: And did you undertake this regression analysis across all companies in the dataset?

Mr G: No. That would have been impracticable. Most companies do not have the right information in the right form to be able to do the kind of analysis we needed to undertake our analysis.

Mr C: I see. Please continue

Mr G: Anyway, as we did more of these analyses we honed down our list of questions that seemed to have the highest level of regression with the business performance measures. Then we added a final criterion. The questions had to be 'actionable'. We did not want questions that just measured emotions like '*Are you proud to be working for your company?*'.

Mr C: Oh, really? I can see why a question like '*Are you proud to be working for your company?*' is not particularly actionable, but I wonder how some of the statements you ended up using are any more actionable, like the one about 'having a best friend at work'?

Mr G: Hmmm... Anyway, to finish the story, having done all sorts of analyses on lots of different surveys we then finally wanted to find out if high scores on our twelve questions were related to more favourable business outcomes across organisations generally. And our correlation analyses suggested that, by and large, they were.

Mr C: I see. And how many companies did you review?

Mr G: In our meta analysis, we used twenty-four in all, but we were able to split these up into around 2,500 business units, although admittedly most of these were retail outlets or branches of financial service organisations.

Mr C: I see. So you then did your correlation analysis and found, what, that the twelve questions that now make up the 'Q12' did appear to be related to business outcomes?

Mr G: Generally, yes, all of the statements correlated positively with at least two of the four business outcome measures.

Mr C: So, does that mean that the presence of these attitudes in the organisation is driving business performance?

Mr G: Well, some might say that, but all we would claim is that there is a link.

Mr C: So you cannot say that these attitudes *drive* organisational performance?

Mr G: No, we cannot.

Mr C: But I guess it could work the other way round?

Mr G: What do you mean?

Mr C: Well, suppose we were a bank. Some branches will be more successful than others for a whole variety of reasons that need have nothing to do with the staff at the branch. They may, for example, be located in areas that are more affluent or better placed for passing footfall in the High Street. Because they are more successful, the bank will invest more in providing better facilities for customers and a better working environment. This will help create more growth, better opportunities for promotion and higher staff bonuses. In those circumstances, you would be likely to record higher overall customer and staff satisfaction and higher scores on all the Gallup 'Q12' questions. But it really has nothing to do with intrinsic staff attitudes, but rather the much more favourable trading circumstances for that branch.

Mr G: I guess you could well be right.

Mr C: So all I really seem to have is another set of performance outcome measures, but nothing that tells me what I need to do to improve them. Nor, indeed, anything that tells me whether they are actually measures I should actually be concerned about.

Mr G: What do you mean?

Mr C: Well, it is a bit like going to a doctor and saying you have a headache. Unless the doctor has more information, he has no idea if the cause is something deadly serious like a brain tumour or something relatively unimportant, like a hangover.

Mr G: I see.

Mr C: If these attitudes are not driving our performance, then they are presumably symptoms of some deeper-rooted causes, but your questionnaire fails to reveal what these are. All I seem to have is a set of measures that echo what we already know from our business outcome measures, but no information I can act on.

Mr G: So how can we help?

Mr C: Well, returning to my original question, what do you suggest we do about our 'below-the-norm' score on the statement relating to how far our supervisors seem to care about our employees?

Best Companies

Its approach

Best Companies Ltd was established in 2000. It positions itself as 'the workplace engagement specialists' with a primary purpose to 'help make the world a better workplace'.[19]

It has become particularly well known through its annually compiled UK list of 'Best Companies to Work For'. Its first list was compiled in 2001. Each year since 2005, the list has been featured in the Sunday Times as 'The Sunday Times 100 Best Companies to Work For' and generates a huge amount of publicity for the companies involved.

The list is based on scores derived at least 90% from an employee survey consisting of around 65-70 statements and a seven-point agree/disagree scale. The questionnaire is self-administered by companies that sign up to the scheme, following Best Companies' prescribed methodology. The remaining up to 10% score is described as 'discretionary' and is derived from a questionnaire filled out by each company.

Best Companies also runs an accreditation scheme. This awards a one, two or three star accreditation to companies according to how they score on the questions. Many of those that receive accreditation take this as a badge of pride and issue press releases to inform the world, and their employees, of their great achievement.

The questions used to evaluate companies and issue accreditations are agree/disagree scale statements. Best Companies spent a great deal of time and effort refining down its list of questions using what it claims was 'an authoritative and highly rigorous methodology'.[20]

This methodology consisted largely of factor analysis designed to identify the core factors in the data. (See p62 for explanation of factor analysis.)

While Gallup claims to have derived its statements from focus groups conducted in hundreds of companies over many years, Best Companies drew on a group of 'experts' to help them compile a list of 134 questions (statements).[21]

The questionnaire was initially administered to around 20,000 employees across various companies. Best Companies then undertook what it refers to as 'exploratory factor analysis' on this data, then a 'confirmatory factor analysis' on the data from a further 50,000 respondents a year later.

This produced eight factors that accounted for most of the variability in the data. Statements that did not contribute to these factors and those that correlated very closely with other statements were eliminated. This left around 65 statements (it varies slightly year on year as new statements are tested and substituted) that are used to calculate the scores for 'The Sunday Times Best 100 Companies to Work For.'

The Best Companies' eight factors

Leadership
How feel about the head of their organisation, senior management team, organisational values

Well being
Stress, pressure, balance between work and home life, impact of these on personal health and performance

Giving something back
How much people think their organisation puts back into society, believe this is driven by profit motive

My manager
Whether feel supported, trusted and cared for by immediate manager

Fair deal
How well employees feel they are treated and how their pay and benefits compare to similar organisations

My team
Encouraging team spirit, feeling part of the organisation, having fun, belonging

Personal growth
Whether people feel challenged by their job, skills utilised, perceived opportunities for advancement

My company
How much people value their organisation, how proud they are to work there, whether they make a difference

To get the score that is used to rank companies in the Sunday Times '100 Best Companies to Work for' listing, it first calculates a score reflecting the response to each statement. This is done by first allocating a value to each of the seven scale points starting with 1 for *'strongly disagree'* ranging through 4 for *'neither agree nor disagree'* and ending with 7 for *'strongly agree'*. (For statements that are phrased negatively the scoring would be the other way round.) The average score across all respondents is then calculated. Thus, if there were exactly 700 respondents and exactly 100 selected each of the seven scale options, then the average score for that statement would be 4. If all 700 responded *'strongly agree'* then the average score would be 7. Far more likely is that a majority would agree, at least with the positively worded statements, to give an average of maybe between 5 and 6.

The scores for all the statements in each factor are then averaged to give overall factor scores. These factor scores are then averaged to give one overall score for the company. However, before this last averaging is done, each factor score is given a weighting according to its 'standard deviation'. Essentially this is a measure of how much the factor score tends to vary between different organisations. The thinking here is that a variable that tends to vary a lot between companies will have much more impact on the overall score than one that only varies a little. This weighting is a way of ensuring that each factor contributes equally to the overall score.

As a result of all this, Best Companies claims that it has developed 'the most accurate and valid survey instrument in the UK for measuring employee attitudes to their work and their organisation'. However, is this really true? What is the basis for such an assertion and does it stand up to close scrutiny?

Critique of the Best Companies' Approach

One can understand the attraction of having a 'universal' set of questions that can be applied to all companies irrespective of their sector, size or individual aspirations. However, I am not convinced it is necessarily a very helpful approach for organisations serious about improving their performance or employee engagement. As with Gallup, there are a number of reasons to be wary of the Best Companies approach.

Agree/disagree statements that only measure attitudes/beliefs

The Best Companies' questionnaire consists almost exclusively of agree/disagree statements. This technique was essentially developed to measure attitudes and is very poor at measuring behaviours, motivations or knowledge.

Moreover, its agree/disagree list of statements is totally standardised. This means that it is not possible to customise the survey to meet the unique needs of each organisation. The inclusion of two open-ended questions is the only concession to those looking to obtain any kind of customised feedback from their staff. On these grounds alone, its claims do not hold much credibility.

The standardised list of statements mean that it is not possible to customise the survey to meet the unique needs of each organisation

Coverage no better than other consultants

In using factor analysis to define and justify the statements, Best Companies has gone out on a limb compared with other consultancies. However, the assumptions underlying factor analysis give rise to a number of questions. The first of these is whether its list of statements is really any better than that of other consultants that have not undertaken such sophisticated statistical analysis.

If we compare the factor titles with the categories used by other consultancies (see table on p127) there is clearly a fair degree of overlap on things like 'personal growth', 'management' and 'teamwork'. However, while the others do not seem to include questions to do with 'giving something back' they do include other items such as 'customer focus' and 'communications' that appear to be missing from the Best Companies list.

While it might defend its approach by saying that it has demonstrated that these statements reflect a deeper structure in the data, I am not convinced that that is a justification for claiming they are a better set of statements than those produced by other companies. If there is a case it is very marginal. The analysis, after all, was done on a very large dataset across many companies; but why should the same structures apply to all, or indeed any, individual company?

Categorisations not best suited to individual companies

Even if we do accept that these structures apply to all organisations, it seems to me that the categorisations that follow from them can get in the way of management being able to draw useful conclusions from the research. Issues need to be dealt with through the established processes and structures of the business and these are unlikely to correspond neatly with the factor categories.

The argument that the real meaning lies in the factors is of little help to management since the meaning of each factor is far from obvious, a fact that Best Companies seems to acknowledge when it says that you do not look at the factors to find out what you should be doing; rather you need to look at the statements that make up the factors. 'The most valuable use of the factor model' it tells us 'is in the structured feedback of survey results to the organisation'. Another way of putting this might be to say that the factor model itself is not very useful for management. Its main purpose was to narrow down the list of statements Best Companies uses for accrediting companies and providing a list of categories for organising the results.

Arguably, though, this is no better a list than you could have compiled yourself. Indeed, it is probably worse since just by looking at what the statements are about you could categorise them to match what you know about the structure and management systems of your organisation.

Exclusion of important questions

Although Best Companies assembled 'experts' to draft its original list of statements, one cannot exclude the possibility that they may have omitted to include certain aspects of the work experience that many people would consider important. The fact that other consultants have included different statements based on their experiences, suggests that the Best Companies list was far from a definitive starting point.

Even if one assumes that the list of statements that Best Companies started out with was an appropriate one, there is still the possibility that the techniques it employed had the effect of excluding some of the most important ones. Many statements would have been excluded, and therefore deemed unimportant, because they did not happen to correlate highly with other statements in the factor analysis.

However, it might be that some of those statements covered issues that employees actually felt very strongly about and which were critical in their evaluation of their employer as an organisation to work for. Because Best Companies only included statements that correlated highly with other statements, these maverick, but nonetheless important, statements would have been excluded.

Because Best Companies only included statements that correlated highly with other statements, these maverick, but nonetheless important, statements would have been excluded

Inability to determine which statements are most important

We highlighted earlier how one of the limitations of agree/disagree scale technique is its inability to determine which statements are more important to respondents than others. Best Companies' view is that its factor analysis determined 'the factors that employees filling in the surveys regard as most important to their engagement'. In my view, it does not. For one thing, they were never given the opportunity to say what was most important to their engagement. For another, I do not accept that correlation necessarily implies importance. While factor analysis will find what variables (statements) correlate most closely together, it makes no judgement as to how important employees consider the issues covered by the statements.

Evaluating the relative importance of statements to employees is generally not relevant where agree/disagree statements are used simply to test hypotheses about what people think about the organisation e.g. do they feel it treats people equally on the grounds of race or gender or do they feel people are penalised for speaking up about things they think are wrong in the organisation? But where the statements are being used to score companies in terms of whether they are deemed to be 'among the best companies to work for' you might expect question techniques to be employed that allowed staff to say what things mattered most to them in their jobs then to rate their employer in terms of those factors.

Despite Best Companies' assertion that the factor analysis 'determines the factors that employees filling in the surveys regard as most important to their engagement', in my view it does not

Unequal weighting given to statements and factors

You might be forgiven for assuming that each statement carries equal weight in the overall and factor scorings. In fact, they do not. The weights vary markedly and relate to the numbers of statements that go to make up each factor. Thus, if a factor summarises a larger number of statements, then each of those statements would contribute less to the overall factor score than if the factor summarises a small number of statements. Indeed, some statements count for up to twice as much as other statements in the overall scoring.

Thus, the relative weightings given to the statements in calculating the scoring for the Sunday Times Best Companies listing, and company accreditation, has nothing to do with the importance attributed to them by employees. Instead, it is determined first by whether the statements correlated highly with any other statements, in which case they were allowed to be included in the calculation, and second by how many other statements were allocated to the same category.

Two things are certain. The first is that people do value some things a lot more in their jobs than other things. The second is that the weightings that the Best Companies' analysis ascribes to the statements is very unlikely to correspond to the relative importance people would ascribe to them if the question format allowed them to.

One implication of this might be that all the scores for the Sunday Times rankings and the Best Companies' accreditations are 'wrong'! However, there is no way of saying how wrong they are. Another is that scoring for the Best Companies' accreditation system may be skewing the results in favour of those companies that do well on things that employees do not care much about, and against those that do well on the things that employees care passionately about.

Failure to accommodate unique nature of individual businesses

A major concern with measuring tools that are used to draw up ranked listings of companies is that the measures totally ignore what the management of those companies are aiming to achieve individually. A medium-sized retailer will have quite different issues to a large law firm, a rail operator different priorities to an airline, and so on. What is important to management and employees in one environment may be of little relevance to those in another environment. The business models are quite different, so why should they be measured using the same measures with the same weightings given to each statement as everyone else? Although the approach meets the objective of producing comparative scores and rankings for Best Companies, it does not produce the best information for companies wishing to improve their performance according to their own business models.

A major concern with measuring tools used to draw up ranked listings of companies, is that the measures ignore what the management of those companies are aiming to achieve

The model is not one that management can use

We note elsewhere how one of the problems of questionnaires made up entirely of agree/disagree statements is getting the data to 'join up' to tell a convincing story of how the organisation works. Factor analysis might appear to provide a solution to this problem. Best Companies, for example, claimed that through its analysis it was able 'to develop a complex statistical model of the workplace' that it refers to as a 'factor model of employee engagement'.

In a purely statistical sense, it has created a model. However, I have difficulty seeing this as a particularly useful model for management. It seems to be stretching a point to call it a 'model of employee engagement'. A model of employee engagement should, to my mind, explain just how the different elements of the working environment work together to create employee engagement and, hopefully, desirable outcomes for the business. However, the factor model fails to do that.

Inactionable results

The Best Companies questionnaire also falls short in terms of actionability. Curiously, its rationale for not including its 'employee engagement construct' (a ninth factor that appears to be derived from statements used in other factors) as one of its core factors was that 'it is not directly actionable'. It is derived from statements such as *'I love working for this organisation'* and *'I feel proud to work for this organisation'*. As it rightly points out, if there is a problem in these areas there is no clear action on how to improve.

It is difficult to see how, what are essentially a series of summarised and unconnected clusters of variables, constitutes a 'model of employee engagement'

However, you could argue that many of the statements that feed into its core factors (and that are used in calculating the Sunday Times list scores) are equally difficult to action. The example it gives of a statement that is actionable is: *'Senior managers of this organisation do a lot of telling and not much listening'*. However, the reality is that it is very far from clear what actions you can take without a lot more information. Moreover, other statements such as *'This organisation is run on strong moral principles'* or *'Senior managers truly live the values of this organisation'* are just as difficult to action as *'I love working for this organisation'*.

Conclusion

Although no doubt well intentioned, one has to conclude that Best Companies' claim to have 'the most accurate and valid survey instrument in the UK for measuring employee attitudes to their work and their organisation' just does not hold up. It falls foul of all the limitations we have outlined in this book of surveys made up of generically phrased agree/disagree scale statements. These limitations are not helped by the application of factor analysis.

Best Companies' claim to have 'the most accurate and valid survey instrument in the UK for measuring employee attitudes to their work and their organisation' just does not hold up

Ironically, though, despite all these criticisms, its surveys probably do impact on organisations in a positive way. Almost without doubt, the process of focusing on the areas that Best Companies uses in its accreditation, and the knowledge of the publicity that will accompany publication of the Best Companies league table, will lead to an improvement in the way many organisations behave towards their own staff, and possibly to an improvement in their performance as a result.

A client's perspective?

Again, you might imagine a conversation between a client and a consultant from Best Companies.

Mr C: Thank you for sending us the survey results for our company. I see we did not make it into the 'Sunday Times'100 Best Companies to Work for'.

Mr B: No. You were pulled down on some scores in particular.

Mr C: Oh, like what?

Mr B: Like 'giving something back'.

Mr C: What does that mean?

Mr B: Well, as you know, we have eight 'factors' that your company is scored on and one you did particularly poorly on was about giving something back to society.

Mr C: Oh, I see. And how are these scores worked out?

Mr B: Well, basically, we calculate scores for each statement that reflect how strongly people agree or disagree with them. The top score is seven, which you would get if everyone strongly agreed with a positive statement. The bottom score is one, which you would get if everyone disagreed with a positive statement, or, indeed, agreed with a negative statement.

Mr C: I see.

Mr B: Then, to get the scores for each factor, like the 'giving something back' factor, we take an average of the scores for the statements that we use to measure that factor.

Mr C: OK. So looking at this list of questions, or should I say 'statements', I can see one here that says *'I think this organisation should put more back into the local community'*. Is that one of the ones that feeds in to the 'giving something back' factor?

Mr B: Yes, I believe it is.

Mr C: So would we get a high or a low score if our employees generally agreed with that?

Mr B: Well, a low score.

Mr C: Oh? Why is that?

Mr B: Because if they think that the company should put more back into the local community, they clearly think it is not doing enough.

Mr C: Or maybe they are just a very altruistic bunch of people who think you can never give too much, particularly as most of our employees come from the local community so I can see that they would always like us to support it more. But if we were based in, say, a very commercial part of a large city or an out-of-town industrial park, where our employees commuted in from all over the place, I can see that our staff would not feel that it was very appropriate for us to 'put more back into the local community', because there wouldn't be one! In that case, our staff would disagree. We would get a high score even though we did very little for the local community. In fact, we do a lot for the local community, but I can see now that we are probably penalised in your scoring system relative to some firms that do far less.

Mr B: Yes, well, maybe the question is not perfect.

Mr C: And what about this one: '*My organisation's support of worthy causes is driven by a desire for good publicity*'. Does that contribute to the same factor?

Mr B: Yes, I believe it does.

Mr C: So, presumably, if our employees generally agree with that, that would give us a low score?

Mr B: Yes, I believe it would.

Mr C: But surely it is not a bad thing to want to be credited with the good work that you do. I can quite see that a lot of our staff would have agreed with that because we do publicise the worthy things we do. We feel this helps others in the community to rally round and support those causes. But I would bet that if you had also put the statement to them that said *'My organisation's support of worthy causes is driven by a desire to improve the world we live in'* most of our employees would have agreed with that too.

Mr B: So what point are you making?

Mr C: Well, I have only looked at two statements so far and, as far as I can see, we have been marked down even though we are a good employer simply because of what you assume our staff are thinking when they answered the questions, although in many cases I am sure you are wrong!

Mr B: Hmmm…

Mr C: So anyway, where did these statements come from?

Mr B: Oh, we asked a group of 'experts' to help us develop them. Originally we had around 134 but we reduced these to around 65.

Mr C: So how did you do that?

Mr B: Well, we applied a statistical technique called 'factor analysis'. What this does is to see what variables, or statements, appear to correlate together best, suggesting that there are underlying 'factors' or basic 'core attitudes' that these statements are measuring.

Mr C: I see.

Mr B: We found that there seemed to be around eight factors that emerged strongly from the analysis. We call this our 'Factor Model of Employee Engagement'. These became the eight Best Companies factors that we use to accredit companies and to identify the Sunday Times list of the 'Best 100 Companies to work for'.

Mr C: So any statements that did not fit in with those factors were dropped?

Mr B: That is correct.

Mr C: Why was that?

Mr B: Well we reckon that if they don't correlate they are unlikely to be tapping in to something that is likely to have a major impact on workplace performance.

Mr C: But could you not have left out some statements that were important to how organisations perform but which just did not happen to correlate with any other statements? Indeed, there may have been statements that were never in the original list that may, in some companies at least, relate to things that are critically important to their performance.

Mr B: Like what?

Mr C: Well, I notice there are no statements relating to 'communications' or to 'customer focus' in your list, yet these have featured in surveys we have seen from other firms. Moreover, although the statements you selected correlated well together, as I understand it, that does not mean that they are necessarily more important to employees than the ones you rejected. Your methodology did not involve any process designed to identify the variables that people considered more or less important to them.

Mr B: True, we did not attempt to measure what employees considered important. We assume that because statements correlate well together, they reflect, if you like, something more meaningful in the organisation than statements that do not correlate.

Mr C: That may be true, but my concern would be that these factors are really measuring similarity of theme rather than deep rooted core attitudes. In other words, you would expect statements about the team people work in to correlate with each other more than with statements about, for example, their pay and benefits or whether they feel their business is 'giving something back'.

Mr B: So how could we have measured how important employees considered each statement?

Mr C: You cannot. We have come across this before. One of the problems of questionnaires that consist solely of agree/disagree statements is that you cannot get employees to prioritise them. It does not make any sense. Anyway, I am still trying to understand your 'Factor Model of Employee Engagement'. From what you describe, it is a 'model' that is derived through statistical analysis.

Mr B: Yes.

Mr C: And, as I understand it, you believe this statistical analysis suggests that there are around eight deep-rooted, 'core attitudes', or 'factors', that we can assume to exist because of the way the agree/disagree statements correlated together.

Mr B: Yes.

Mr C: So how does that help me?

Mr B: What do you mean?

Mr C: Well, can you tell me more about these 'core attitudes'?

Mr B: Like what?

Mr C: Like how they link to our business performance, or how I can influence them to improve our performance.

Mr B: Well, not really.

Mr C: You see, this 'model' is all a bit abstract to me. What I need is hard information that feeds into a model that I can recognise as a reasonable representation of how my business works. Knowing that there are, or may be, some core deep-rooted attitudes in the workforce, (but not specifically my workforce!), that can be measured by a number of attitude statements that were not really devised for my workforce anyway, is not very helpful to me.

Mr B: Well, we reckon that if you get high scores on these factors then your staff will be more engaged and your business will perform better.

Mr C: But surely, you could say that about any number of agree/disagree statements drawn from different consultancies. It seems to me that if you cover off the main aspects of the business, like how line managers behave towards their staff, and the factors driving job satisfaction such as pay and benefits, career development and training, and so on, then you could come up with an equally good set of measures.

Mr B: Well that is your view.

Mr C: But even then, I have a problem.

Mr B: And what is that?

Mr C: Well, whether the statements come from you or from another consultancy, I have a real difficulty with answers that give me nothing substantial to which to respond.

Mr B: Can you give me an example?

Mr C: Yes, 30% of our employees apparently agree that '*I feel that I lack support from my manager*'.

Mr C: So why do you have a difficulty?

Mr B: Because I have no idea what kind of support they feel they are lacking.

Mr B: I see what you mean.

Mr C: So where do we go from here?

Mr B: Well, maybe you would like to sign up for next year's survey!

The enslavement of engagement

Both Gallup and Best Companies are looking for engaged employees. Buckingham and Coffman say they 'were looking for those special questions where the most engaged employees answered positively and everyone else answered neutrally or negatively'.[22] Best Companies claim to have developed a 'Factor Model of Employee Engagement'. Moreover, they are not the only ones to have latched on to this relatively new idea but one that seems to have taken firm root in the HR function of most major organisations.

I believe that the notion of 'employee engagement' is enormously important. It seems to have come to prominence in HR at the end of the 1990s. However, although it has become a favourite topic for articles and conferences and a focus for many a consultant's offerings, there does not seem to be a consistent definition of what it is.

To me it is about employees being involved in a very positive way with what their organisation is about. Engagement and great leadership have always gone together and, in that respect, it is something that has been around as long as civilisation. On the other hand, it is also understandable why it has become a major focus of 21st century people management. Now, more than at any other time, economic value is created through the provision of services rather than the manufacture and trading of tangible goods. This requires a far greater degree of interaction between people in different organisations. Organisations are also far larger and more complex than in the past. They depend more than ever on very high levels of trust between staff at all levels. Technology has transformed the amount of information within organisations and access to it at all levels. This reinforces the need for increased trust and undermines the 'command and control' systems of ancient armies and not so ancient mass production factories.

In developed economies, people are also far better educated both through the formal education systems and through the mass media – print, broadcast and internet. This means that they are generally much more able to see things from different points of view, adapt to changing situations, and pick up new skills than they were before.

Major organisations are now very complex systems with millions of individual decisions being made every second across every level. What makes them work is the ability for everyone involved to engage with what they are about and to feel motivated, empowered and directed to contribute towards their overall success. An organisation with high employee engagement is an energised organisation. It is one that generates and harnesses the natural, positive human energy and the human spirit.

Diagrammatically, this is how I see employee engagement:

Model of Employee Engagement

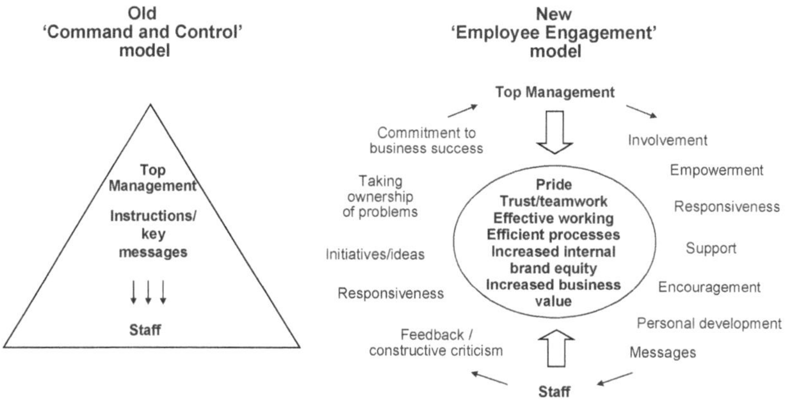

Old 'Command and Control' model

Top Management

Instructions/ key messages

Staff

New 'Employee Engagement' model

Top Management

Commitment to business success

Involvement

Empowerment

Taking ownership of problems

Pride
Trust/teamwork
Effective working
Efficient processes
Increased internal brand equity
Increased business value

Responsiveness

Support

Initiatives/ideas

Responsiveness

Encouragement

Personal development

Feedback / constructive criticism

Messages

Staff

Employee engagement is something that is systemic and cultural and as such ought to be a key concern of those who undertake employee surveys. And, indeed, this appears to be the case. All the major consultancies working in this area talk about 'employee engagement' and most place it central to their thinking, or at least they say they do in their promotional statements. However, are they really talking about 'employee engagement' or is it just a convenient hook on which to hang their wares?

All the major consultancies working in this area talk about 'employee engagement'. But is it really just a convenient hook on which to hang their wares?

Most of the leading employee research consultancies claim, in one way or another, that greater employee engagement will result in better business performance and that their measures are the key to understanding it. Gallup claims that high scores on its 12 questions indicates a company whose employees are 'the most engaged' and that these measures also correlate with the performance of the business. Best Companies claims that its 'Employee Engagement construct' (derived from its agree/disagree scale measures) is 'an excellent measure of the performance of any given organisation'. Watson Wyatt claims to have discovered four key areas that need managing in order to achieve 'engagement' that in turn drives performance. Towers Perrin/ISR claims that 'employee engagement affects key business outcomes such as sales, customer satisfaction and employee turnover'. And so on.

However, none of them provides any convincing empirical proof that high employee engagement does drive performance, nor that their measures are the best ones to help organisations manage their engagement.

I have little doubt that high employee engagement does drive performance. It seems self-evident that people who are more committed, empowered, respected, motivated and energised will perform better than those who are uncommitted, powerless, disrespected, de-motivated and de-energised. However, I am not convinced that any of the questions that leading consultancies claim can help us manage employee engagement stand up to close scrutiny.

None of them provides any convincing proof that ... their measures are the best ones to help organisations manage their engagement

It seems to me that employee engagement is something that should be reflected in every aspect of the way people relate to the organisations they work for. Truly engaged people engage with their organisation's management, internal systems and communication, core thinking such as its values, vision, and mission, its customers and other stakeholders, and also with their inner self and their own personal values and needs that they seek to fulfil at work. In that respect, every question in an employee questionnaire should give you some insight into the nature of employee engagement – even agree/disagree scale questions.

The main problem with agree/disagree scales in this respect is, though, that they are limited in what they can effectively measure. As we have seen, they are very poor at measuring behaviours, motivations and knowledge and in getting the data to join up in a coherent way. The failure of many consultants to customise their questions for individual organisations imposes another major constraint on their ability to understand employee engagement in any particular organisation.

The failure of many consultants to customise their questions for individual organizations, imposes another major constraint on their ability to understand employee engagement in any particular organisation

The Towers Perrin/ISR model is typical of this approach. It sees engagement as critical to achieving 'key business outcomes such as sales, customer satisfaction and employee turnover'.[23] It postulates a framework that it calls the 'ISR Engagement Model'. This has three components, or factors, that influence engagement. These are:

1. **Cognitive (Thinking)**: Cognitive commitment is said to occur when employees agree with the organisation's goals and values and decide to support them.

2. **Affective (Feelings):** Truly engaged employees feel a sense of belonging and attachment in their organisation.

3. **Behavioural (Actions)**: This is expressed in employees' willingness to act in ways that are consistent with their beliefs and feelings and has two facets: their willingness to stay with the organisation and their willingness to put in extra effort.

Strong employee engagement, it claims, comes from a combination of all three. Measuring all three is necessary both to understand the current level of engagement and to develop appropriate improvement initiatives.

On the face of it, this seems a sensible framework. Unfortunately, though, the framework is let down by the research tools – agree/disagree scale questions – that are supposed to support it.

One core output from ISR's research for its clients is an Employee Engagement Index. This is calculated by averaging the percentage agreeing with each of six statements, two representing each of the three components of the Engagement Model.

On the face of it, this seems a sensible framework. Unfortunately, it is let down by the agree/disagree scale questions that are supposed to support it

If we take the statements used in this Index, we can see how it comes unstuck. Under the Cognitive component, the statements are along the lines of:

'I believe strongly in the goals and objectives of [Employer]'

and

'I fully support the values for which [Employer] stands'

The trouble with each of these is that they really measure attitudes rather than (cognitive) thinking. They both assume that staff know what the questions refer to. The reality in most companies is that there is a lot of confusion in employees' minds, and for good reason. Often different parts of the company – e.g. different divisions, or subsidiaries or teams – have their own goals and values; or companies frequently develop them, but do not refer to them as 'goals' or 'values'. Moreover, even if they have developed these at senior management level, they are often poorly communicated down to more junior staff. Consequently, the response to statements such as these do not really reflect how far employees 'agree with the organisation's goals and values' and the extent to which they have 'decided to support them'. Rather it measures a combination of:

- Acknowledged ignorance (I don't know what the goals and values are so I will either say I 'disagree' with the statements or that I 'neither agree nor disagree')

- Confusion (I think I know what they are talking about so will answer on that basis, even though, unbeknown to me, the question is actually referring to something quite different) and
- Informed judgement (I understand correctly what the question is about and respond accordingly)

Unfortunately, the flaw in these questions undermines the robustness of the Employee Engagement Index and highlights one of the dangers of using indices compiled by combining or averaging a number of different variables.

A far better way of asking the questions would be to state what you are talking about e.g. the company's value statement, then to ask employees first, whether they have ever seen or heard that statement before and then how far they support it. In the latter case, this could be expressed in a number of ways. For example you might ask how far staff feel personally committed to the values, how far they feel the values are appropriate ones for the company, how far they feel their managers live them and so on. However, you cannot do this, at least not elegantly, using the agree/disagree scale question format.

The Action component of the model falls down because the statements used actually measure attitudes not behaviours. The statements are:

> *'I work beyond what is required to help [Employer] succeed'*
>
> and
>
> *'At the present time are you seriously considering leaving [Employer]?'*

To be fair to ISR, it does define the Action component in terms of *willingness to act* in certain ways, rather than actual behaviours, but this is somewhat at odds with the model that makes a clear distinction between attitudes and behaviours.

The two statements that relate to the Feeling component of the Model are along the lines of:

> *'I would recommend [Employer] as a good place to work'*
>
> and
>
> *'I am proud to be a part of [Employer]'*

Both attitude statements provide good overall measures of how employees feel about their employer. However, it is, in my view, wrong to think that six questions together, or indeed the whole battery of core questions it uses in its questionnaires – that can easily run to 60 or more statements – adequately fulfils the criteria that its corporate literature claims it is meant to, specifically: 'to understand both what the current level of engagement is, and to develop appropriate improvement initiatives'.

If you want to do this, it is necessary to break out of the agree/disagree scale straightjacket. Understanding why staff believe the company they work for is 'a good place to work' is far more likely to come from questions that explore the work experience in ways other than agreement with a range of attitude statements. Asking staff, for example, what would make them recommend their employer (if they do not) or recommend it more strongly (if they do) will provide much greater insight into the issues the company needs to address to improve engagement than poring over the results of scores of attitude statements.

To understand the current level of engagement, and develop appropriate improvement initiatives, it is necessary to break out of the agree/disagree scale straightjacket

Moreover, if we accept the basic 'Engagement Model' and its three components – thinking, feelings, actions - then relying on a research technique that is very poor at measuring behaviours, motivations and knowledge, would seem a misguided approach.

As we have seen, Best Companies developed a 'Factor Model of Employee Engagement'. However, there is no definition of 'employee engagement' or any explanation of how these factors are supposed to work to produce employee engagement. Enigmatically, it also refers to a ninth factor, or 'construct', that it actually labels 'employee engagement'. According to Best Companies, this factor is 'an excellent measure of the performance of any given organisation'.

However, there is no objective verification of this. In other words, the statistical analysis presented is all about deriving the eight, or nine, factors. It is not about demonstrating that these factors in any way drive organisational or business performance in terms of, for example, growth, profitability, efficiency and so on. We are left to take it as a given that engagement is a good thing and that the eight factors tell us what we should be focusing on to increase engagement.

The models and measures promoted by leading consultancies offering employee surveys are therefore seriously underwhelming. 'Employee engagement', as used by various consultancies, appears to be no more than a convenient label linking their analyses to a term that is widely used by, and has positive connotations for, HR managers. If management wants to use research as a tool to help increase employee engagement - and it should – then it first needs to develop a clear understanding of what employee engagement is and how it believes it should work in their organisation. Its employee survey should then be designed to fit this model. It should not just adopt a consultancy's model without questioning its robustness and appropriateness for what it is trying to do.

'Employee engagement', as used by various consultancies, appears to be no more than a convenient label linking their analyses to a term that is widely used by HR managers

PART 3

Doing it right

PART 3: Doing it right

Asking the right questions

Questionnaire design is critical to a successful employee survey. Good questions yield insights that enable you to make better decisions for the benefit of management, staff and the organisation as a whole. Poor questions can simply fail to provide any useful information or, worse, mislead you into focusing on the wrong issues and making the wrong decisions.

There is no absolute right or wrong way of designing an employee questionnaire, though there are good and bad practices. In the opening section, I outlined a list of different types of questions that can be used in employee surveys with examples of where they could be applied. In my view, the best questionnaires are ones that start with the company's business plan or success model: Where is it trying to go? How is it trying to get there? What issues is it trying to address? They then adopt the most appropriate types of questions to generate the best information for feeding into planning and decision-making.

There is no absolute right or wrong way of designing an employee questionnaire, though there are good and bad practices

Top management will usually have some notion of the kind of organisation they want to have and some ideas of the major issues they need to address that relate to their employees. There will also be many individuals throughout the organisation who have their own ideas of issues they feel need to be addressed to make it a better place to work and more effective at achieving its goals. One key to developing the right questionnaire for your business is to ensure the right process is employed to ensure that it reflects its unique needs. This argues against adopting a standard set of agree/disagree statements that were never originally developed for your organisation and that focus exclusively on measuring attitudes.

Ideally, management should work closely with a researcher who is not only experienced in the finer arts of questionnaire design, but who is a specialist in employee surveys and one who understands management. What you do not want is a 'researcher' who is really only experienced in managing the process of data collection using a standardised questionnaire.

That researcher should be enabled to enter into a dialogue with the main stakeholders in the organisation in order to become familiar with the issues it faces so they can develop questions that will help management understand these better. Sometimes qualitative research (depth interviews or focus groups among staff) can be helpful.

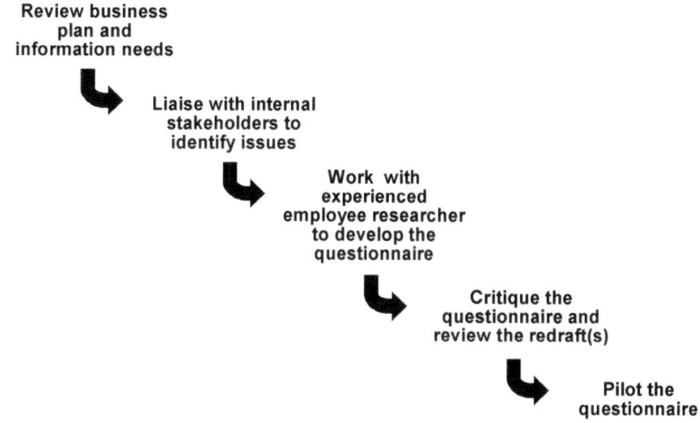

It is also best practice to pilot the questionnaire on a few employees at different levels across the organisation. Pilots should not be a data gathering exercise to see if the answers look sensible and whether any questions generate lots of 'don't know' responses. Rather they should explore what respondents understand by the various questions, to ensure the questions are understood as intended, and whether there are any key areas that have been overlooked.

The questionnaire drafts should be discussed with, and critiqued by, the internal sponsors. In particular, they should be asking themselves whether each question will provide them with information they can do something with. It is not enough for the findings simply to be interesting; they have to tell you something that enables you to move the organisation forward.

What to do with the findings

Having undertaken your employee survey, it is important to involve staff in the process of responding to the findings. Not only are they often able to suggest useful ways forward but, having assured them how important their views are when seeking their participation, it sends a bad signal if they are not involved in some way in addressing issues raised, and an even worse signal if they are never told the outcome of the survey.

An Action Matrix, plotting issues covered in the questionnaire according to their relative importance to staff by how highly the company is rated, can be very useful tool for management and a good focus for team meetings and action planning workshops.

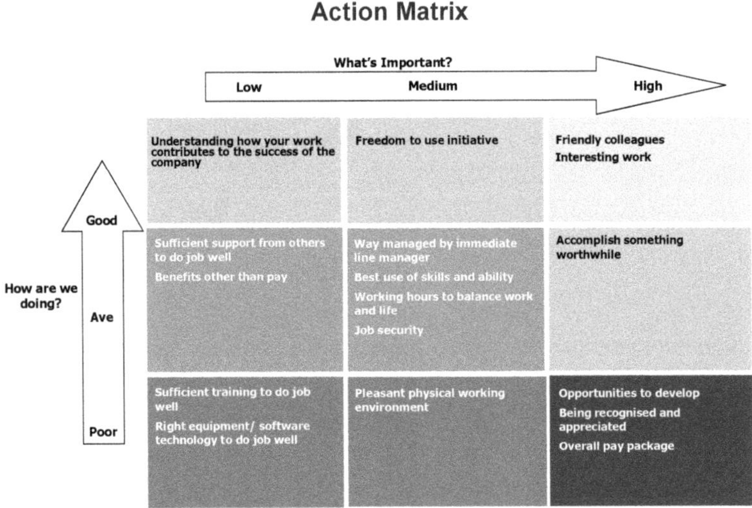

Such matrices are difficult to construct, though, using only agree/disagree question data since the question format does not allow respondents to say which factors are more or less important to them. This severely limits the efficacy of your action planning workshops.

Some agencies claim they can derive 'importance' from regression analysis. However, I find this very unconvincing. The statements were not designed with this kind of analysis in mind; importance ought to be a cognitive concept not a statistical one and the results I have seen are difficult to make sense of.

The workshop efficacy is further limited by the use of standardised agree/disagree statements. Since these were not specifically designed for your company, they are unlikely to get to the heart of what management should be focusing on. Rather than focusing on how to address the issues raised by the research, the workshops are likely to be spent trying to understand how employees interpreted the questions!

If the right questions are asked, then management or internal working parties can focus on how to address the issues raised by the responses. A list of possible actions can be drawn up which then need to be evaluated. Sometimes it is helpful to consider the likely cost and disruption or 'pain' that the organisation will need to bear if each proposal is implemented. The 'Worcester Cost/Pain Matrix' can be a useful management tool. List the possible actions (here represented by 1-25) then plot them according to their likely cost and pain. Low cost, low pain actions are likely to be quick wins. Higher cost and higher pain actions need to be considered more carefully.

Worcester Cost/Pain Matrix

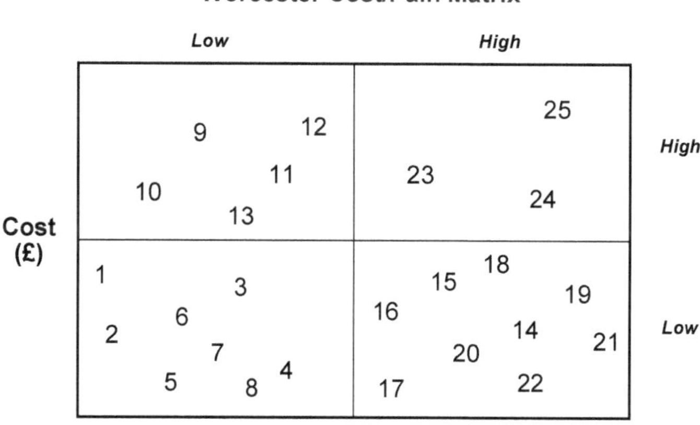

Making sense of it all

My first boss in research, Bob Worcester, founder of the research agency, MORI, used to say that research is a very simple thing: all you have to do is ask the right questions of the right people and add up the results correctly. As I have tried to show in this book, there is more to questionnaire design than drafting a list of statements, or worse still, trotting out a standardised list and asking employees to say how strongly they agree or disagree with them. The danger is that, once the results arrive, attention focuses on the numbers and whether the questions actually mean anything sensible or useful in the particular organisation can get overlooked. Statistical analysis can so often be used to cover up poor questionnaire design and create a reality that obscures rather than reveals what staff are trying to tell you. Numbers can be seductive. Without care, they can take on a life of their own that is so far removed from what was intended by those who answered the questions, as to be worthless as a tool of management. They can end up betraying all the people who took the time to fill out the questionnaire in the belief that management was genuinely interested in their views.

Numbers can be seductive. Without care, they can take on a life of their own that is so far removed from what was intended by those who answered the questions, as to be worthless as a tool of management

Despite what some consultants imply, the questions you ask can only capture a very small part of the overall picture of how organisations work. One type of question is not enough to provide you with the depth and breadth of understanding you need to manage the organisation effectively. Statistical multivariate analyses on large datasets will rarely, if ever, reveal profound but hidden truths that have somehow eluded everyone else. Organisations that perform best are not generally ones that aspire to score highly on a standardised set of agree/disagree statement norms.

Statistical multivariate analyses on large datasets will rarely, if ever, reveal profound but hidden truths that have somehow eluded everyone else

The reality is that, as researchers, all we really have is a set of tools that enable us to systematically ask people a variety of questions, compile the results and interpret the data. What we do not know and cannot find out is far greater than what we do know and can find out. The tools we use are many and varied. Some are suitable for exploring one set of issues, others for other issues. Just as you would not think of constructing a table using just a hammer, so you should not think of constructing an employee questionnaire using just an agree/disagree scale. Each question type and formulation will give you a different insight into how an organisation works.

Organisations are complex human systems. What questionnaires do is allow you to gain lots of insights into how those systems work. However, you still have to put these insights together with whatever else you know about the organisation to build a picture of what is going on. One analogy is to imagine that you are looking at a large ocean liner, but you do not know it is a large ocean liner, or even what an ocean liner is. Each question is like a porthole that allows you to see one small part of the liner. It might be a bit of the bridge or a cabin or the engine room or rudder. The more information you get, the more you can start to speculate about how the bits come together as a whole and how they work. To do this, you need to bring to bear other knowledge, theories or ideas that help you to understand what the liner is, how it works and how to make it work better.

You should also recognise that the organisation is not a closed system. Indeed, its whole purpose is rooted externally as part of a wider society and community. Every organisation has a purpose that has to do with delivering goods or services to particular groups of external stakeholders, not least customers. It is also there to create value, not just in an economic sense, but also in an experiential sense, and not just for shareholders, but for all its stakeholders. The economic value that is created is all ultimately dependent on the creation of non-economic value; in other words on the creation of experiences that people value and are willing to pay for, either in cash or in providing their labour.

While what we might call 'employee engagement' is a critical factor in the value creation process - and therefore a critical asset of the business - it is only one element in a more complex system that needs to embrace other stakeholders and also the tangible assets of the business.

While what we might call 'employee engagement' is a critical factor in the value creation process, it is only one element in a more complex system

Employee surveys should be used to generate an authentic insight into how the people side of the business works to create value. To do this, they need to use questioning techniques that allow them to delve into the undercurrents of people's motivations and the barriers that are stopping them working most effectively. The standardised formulations of the agree/disagree statements too often act as a filter that excludes most of what employees would like to say about their working environment and forces the rest through a distorting lens.

Despite their claims, many consultancies' survey questions are not immediately actionable, especially if they were not devised specifically with your organisation in mind.

When Allan Leighton became chairman of Royal Mail, one of the first things he was faced with was a demoralised workforce. When he asked postmen, who are the backbone of the service, what issues they had, it was not the pay or the hours. Rather it was the fact that the Royal Mail had appointed a new supplier of footwear that made their feet sore, their waterproofs were not robust enough to cope with heavy rain

The standardised formulations of the agree/disagree statements too often act as a filter that excludes most of what employees would like to say

and the bags that they carried their mail in leaked. You can imagine that if they had completed a questionnaire consisting only of agree/disagree statements, they may well have expressed disagreement with statements suggesting that they had the right equipment to do their job, that their supervisor cared about them as a person or that their fellow employers were committed to quality. However, none of these questions in any way points towards the underlying issues.

Questionnaires should be listening devices, and ideally fairly sensitive listening devises, that allow you to pick up on issues that are getting in the way of running the organisation effectively. Not 'having the right equipment to do the job' is not an issue that can be dealt with. Knowing that your key workers have inadequate clothing to perform effectively is. The advantage of working with researchers to develop your own bespoke questionnaire is that you can use it to identify the issues that are stopping your own unique organisation perform most effectively and to test relevant hypotheses that you have about your organisation at that moment.

Questions should not be there essentially to feed consultancies' databanks

Questions should not be there essentially to feed consultancies' databanks. In part, they should be there to provide measures of success, but as much as anything, they should be challenging management's preconceptions about the business, how it works and what drives it, and providing it with the information it needs to make the organisation work better.

I have made much of the use and abuse of multivariate analysis by employee research consultants. This is not a criticism of the statisticians, nor of the researchers; if you have a dataset you may as well try different analyses to see what you might get out of them. But you need to be careful. Do not fall into the trap of believing that what comes out of the analysis is the reality rather than what was put into it.

Do not fall into the trap of believing that what comes out of the analysis is the reality rather than what was put into it

Statistical analysis is very precise. All it works on is numbers that you provide. It has no regard for the meaning of any of the variables you feed into it, nor of the interpretation you choose to put on it. It is also driven by very strict rules. These are not the same rules as govern the behaviours, attitudes, feelings and motivations of the people who fill out the questionnaire. As we have seen, although movements in one variable may be *associated* with movements in another variable, that does not mean that movements in one *cause* movements in the other. Indeed, the whole idea of causation is highly problematical in the social sciences. In complex systems, what generally happens is that you need a number of things to work together in order for things to happen. It is not unlike the weather. The wind 'causes' the clouds to move but the temperature creates the wind by changing the air pressure, but land masses affect how all of these behave and the clouds only exist so long as the temperature and humidity allow the precipitation of water droplets into the atmosphere. In an organisation, for things to happen, arguably, you need the vision, but you also need the direction, the resources, the skills, the commitment, the motivation and the incentives. Some things might be 'drivers' that move things forward, others are facilitators that are necessary for things to happen, others are outcomes or symptoms of what is going on.

Very often, what agree/disagree scale questions are measuring are attitudinal symptoms of what is going on in the organisation, but not ones that point towards any particular drivers or facilitators that are creating the problem. Low agreement scores on '*Profit is the only thing driving this organisation*' or '*I am bored with the work I do*' gives you precious little clue as to what the underlying issues are that need to be addressed. Yet one consultancy presents these as two of the key questions that are supposed to be measuring 'critical factors in the workplace'.

Making it join up

In a typical employee survey, anything from 50 to 150 questions are likely to be asked, whatever types of questions are used. The trouble is, most questions, and particularly agree/disagree statements, only measure one thing at a time. The major challenge is to try to make the questions, or rather the answers to the questions, join up so that they tell a coherent story of what is going on in the organisation.

Most questionnaires cover a number of different facets of the employees' experience. The questionnaires will normally be organised into topic areas reflecting these facets. In interpreting the results, you will generally look at all the questions on, say, communications or line management together to see what conclusions can be drawn. Here are some of the categories that have been used by different consultancies that undertake employee surveys:

Consultancy A	Consultancy B	Consultancy C	Consultancy D
Work organisation Leadership Supervision Teamwork Empowerment Communication Training & development Performance management Career planning Pay and benefits Job satisfaction Employee engagement Organisation image & competitive position External customer focus Internal customer focus Organisation culture	Leadership of employer Employee relations Our customers Your management Equal opportunities Employee communications Performance Reward and recognition Learning and skills Your safety	Job role Progression Communication Consultation Engagement strategy Manager Team working Miscellaneous	Identification Equity Equality Consensus Instrumentality Rationality Development Group dynamics Internationalisation

If you want to make links between different measures, it helps if the questions are constructed to provide a common context in which the different aspects of the topic can be considered together. For example, if you ask a question that says *'Please choose from this list the six items that are most important to you in your job'*, all the items link together under a common theme – the things people look for in a job. The question provides the context for them to do so. You can compare one item in the list with another in terms of their perceived importance. Alternatively, if you ask people to rate their manager according to a list of criteria, or to rate the acceptability of different channels of communication for receiving information about the business, the questions have provided the framework and context to enable the answers to one item to be compared with the responses to another, to link them together.

Unfortunately, if you have defaulted to placing all your questions in an agree/disagree scale format, that option is not open to you. Instead of providing a common context for the statements, the only thing the statements have in common is the agree/disagree scale. Thus, if we take these three statements:

> *'My work is stimulating'*
>
> *'I feel my job is secure'*
>
> *'My work interferes with my responsibilities at home'*

all you really end up with is three lots of answers to three questions that do not relate to each other. You can overcome this lack of context by providing a contextual explanation in the question, e.g., *'How strongly you agree or disagree with the following statements* <u>*about your job*</u>*?'*. However, that is rarely done and, where it is, the statements are not usually phrased in terms that can be readily compared.

An alternative way of asking the question is to ask employees to say how satisfied or dissatisfied they are with each aspect of their job on a five-point, satisfaction scale, changing the phrasing to something like *'Having stimulating work'*, *'Job security'* and *'Achieving a good balance between my home and my work life'*. In this way, all the items are placed in the same framework and can be compared with each another.

If your entire questionnaire is made up of agree/disagree statements, it is quite difficult to make it look as if the output is much more than a lot of independent measures that don't really join up. Some consultants turn to multivariate analyses to try to find a way in which the statements relate to one another statistically. From this, they hope to draw inferences about the business and perhaps to provide frameworks within which to view the research findings. As we have seen, though, this can actually make the problem worse and lead to all sorts of erroneous conclusions being drawn.

Developing frameworks

Having frameworks to understand what employee surveys are saying about your organisation, though, is important. Indeed, usually without realising it, we invoke frameworks to try to make sense of research findings. If we see a finding that says that 50% of staff agree that '*I am under so much pressure I cannot concentrate*' this might trigger a picture of an organisation with groups of staff being harassed by overworked managers, inadequate back-up and resources and people going off sick all the time adding to the general pressure.

Similarly, widespread agreement with the statement '*My manager cares about me as an individual*' might trigger images of a relaxed environment with proper planning, clear expectations, regular meetings, adequate resources and plenty of opportunities for job and career development. Without realising it, we are making assumptions about the way the organisation works that goes far beyond what the one research finding is telling us. These act as frameworks to help us make sense of the research findings.

You could say that that is what research findings are meant to do, to help us to build up a picture of what is going on. However, it is easy to get to a point of confusion, particularly if all your data is attitudinal and you are faced with hundreds of statements, each with different meanings and often triggering apparently contradictory images. Moreover, the picture that is triggered in your mind is likely to be different to the pictures that are triggered in your colleagues' minds.

This is where it is very useful to have more formally developed frameworks that management can build a consensus around and use to develop its response to any survey.

Most helpfully, these frameworks will reflect the systemic nature of the organisation

Most helpfully, these frameworks will reflect the systemic nature of the organisation. Employee surveys, in my view, become most valuable when you view them as providing insights into how different bits of the system are working. Frameworks may attempt to be holistic, capturing how lots of different aspects of the organisation work together within its unique environment to achieve its overall purpose and objectives. Alternatively, they may just capture a small part of the overall system such as the appraisal system or internal communications. If this is the case, then they should plausibly relate to a bigger picture, not stand in isolation purporting to represent a part of the system while actually being based on assumptions that are at odds with the way the system as a whole works.

There are (at least) five places you might take these frameworks from:

- **Employee research consultants**
- **Academic sources**
- **Your own business models and plans**
- **Your own experience, intuition and imagination**
- **Facilitated bespoke framework**

Frameworks from research consultants

Most employee research consultancies have some kind of model or theoretical frameworks behind them, though rarely are these made explicit. They are much more likely to be implied by general statements in their promotional literature than presented in substantial, well thought through and empirically supported papers.

Most consultancies that undertake employee surveys have some kind of model or theoretical frameworks behind them, though rarely are these made explicit

Often it is left up to their clients to derive what these models are by looking at the consultancies' questions. Usually the assumption is that companies that score highly on these questions will perform well as businesses; those that do not will perform poorly. For example, if the consultancy asks people to rate how satisfied they are with their employer as a place to work, you might imply that they have a model that goes something like this: Staff who are more satisfied will be better motivated to do a good job, more committed to the organisation and more likely to work productively, resulting in better business performance. Thin, it might be, but often this is the best you will get!

Theoretical models that are presented are rarely well grounded in organisational theory or supported by empirical proof that they work. More often than not, they come across as 'frameworks of convenience' that link the consultancy's measures to improved performance because that is what their clients want to hear, not because it is necessarily true! Those that rely on agree/disagree scale surveys are particularly prone to this since the question formulation excludes many types of questions that would make their diagnoses more complete with a more direct link from the research findings to likely performance improvements.

More often than not, the theoretical models come across as 'frameworks of convenience' that link the consultancy's measures to improved performance because that is what their clients want to hear

Some consultancies have produced copious papers and even books in support of their frameworks. However, because their data is based only on agree/disagree attitude statements and fail to address any of the non-attitudinal factors (internal and external) that determine how organisations perform, these feel more like justifications for the methodologies and questions they are locked in to than well-grounded attempts to understand how organisations work.

Consultancies that are wedded to the agree/disagree scale often overlook the fact that all they are measuring is attitudes, not the things that generate those attitudes. Thus, although their questionnaires may contain statements about management, teamwork, communications and training, they rarely acknowledge that what they are measuring are the attitudinal symptoms of how management structures, processes, programmes, and so on, are working. Models derived solely from contemplating these attitude measures fail to grasp how organisations work.

Some consultancies appear so fixated with attitude measurement that they overlook the fact that all they are measuring is attitudes, not the things that generate those attitudes

Gallup for example, claims to have discovered the questions that 'capture the *most* information and the most *important* information' about the strength of your workplace. However, there are only 12 questions! Moreover, as we have seen, although it conducted extensive statistical analysis to boil down hundreds of statements to just 12, the frameworks that go with it are very weak. Its main premise, and the focus of all its analysis, is the idea that the main driver of performance is attracting and retaining 'loyal and productive staff'. If you have any other model of what determines organisational performance, then this approach is not for you! At a more general level, the 'Gallup School of Management' has come up with theoretical constructs that it defines as four 'camps'.[24] Into these four camps, it slots its 12 questions (items 2-13 – item 1 is a five-point, job satisfaction scale question that is always asked with the 'Q12'):

Base Camp: 'What do I get?'

Item2: Know what is expected

Item 3: Materials/equipment

Camp 1: 'What do I give?'

Item 4 Opportunity to do what I do best

Item 5 Recognition/praise

Item 6 Cares about me

Item 7 Encourages development

Camp2: 'Do I belong?'

Item 8 Opinions count

Item 9 Mission/purpose

Item 10 Committed/quality

Item 11 Best friend

Camp 3: 'How can we grow?'

Item 12 Talked about progress

Item 13 Opportunities to learn

One can see a vague logic behind these classifications, though one has to wonder about the appropriateness of the labels. Camp 1, for example, is labelled 'What do I give?' and yet the four items (5-7) are all about what they receive. Camp 2 is labelled 'Do I belong?' yet Item 10 refers to their associates being committed to doing quality work, which seems to have little to do with whether the respondents feel that they belong. Camp 3 is labelled 'How can we grow?' yet the items only relate to the growth of the individual, not the business. Base Camp is labelled 'What do I get?', but the one thing that everyone comes to work for, pay, is missing. So although the framework seems to have a 'psychological contract' feel about it, it does not seem to fit the measures it is supposed to explain, a lot of important things that we know employees value in the workplace are missing altogether, and it is entirely attitudinally based.

Although the framework seems to have a 'psychological contract' feel about it, it does not seem to fit the measures it is supposed to explain

Similarly, as we saw earlier, Towers Perrin/ISR has developed an 'Engagement Model' that again fails to look beyond what are essentially attitudes in the workplace.

Watson Wyatt claims that surveys are essentially about measuring employee attitudes and opinions and has developed an Employee Effectiveness Model. In its view, the focus should 'no longer be about employee satisfaction' but rather 'commitment and engagement' as it believes these drive performance. In its model, 'commitment' and 'line of sight' – which is about understanding where the organisation is going – together deliver 'true engagement'. Also needed are 'enablement' – essentially training, tools and resources to do the job – and 'integrity' – understanding and living the corporate values, trust in leadership etc.

It has its own employee research tool to measure the 'key indictors' and the 'drivers' of these four areas. However, these measures all appear to be agree/disagree scale questions. Although it presents a model that links 'culture' and 'people practices' as 'drivers' with outputs of 'customer satisfaction' and 'productivity' resulting in 'company performance', with only employee attitudes at its core, the 'model' lacks credibility.

One consultancy that does appear to have a sensible framework is Mercer. Its Human Capital Strategy Six Factor Model defines factors that go way beyond mere attitudes.[25]

Its factors are defined as:

People - capabilities, training & education, demographics

Work processes – work flows, sequencing of activities, division of labour, unit interdependencies

Managerial structures - roles and responsibilities, job design, reporting relationship and requirements, goal specification, performance management

Information and knowledge – communication mechanism and flows, information exchange, intellectual capital use/creation, information systems

Decision-making – vision/strategy, decision-making accountability, speed and quality of decision-making, participation, decentralisation

Rewards – monetary/non-monetary, long-/short term, the work itself, career progression

Mercer's Human Capital Strategy Six factor Model

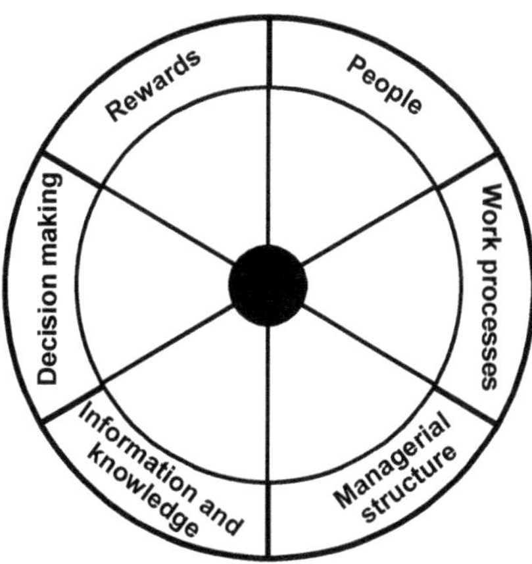

Overall, though, most consultancies promoting employee surveys do not have an approach that is well grounded in organisational theory. Even those that appear to have more robust theoretical models behind them are disappointingly inclined to default to the agree/disagree scale measures to populate their models.

Even those that appear to have more robust theoretical models behind them are disappointingly inclined to default to the agree/disagree scale measures to populate their models

For those without theoretical models, there is a kind of implied model that emerges from the categories of questions that they include in their surveys. These appear to recognise that most employees in any organisation want to be recognised, appreciated and rewarded and many want to develop their skills and their careers. Managers need to get the best out of their staff while delivering the business goals/objectives. In order to do so they need to treat their staff with respect, listen to them and help them develop their talents. Structures and systems need to enable staff to do their jobs effectively and make them feel involved and engaged with the organisation, and so on.

One model that I was involved in validating has proved quite useful. It was developed by organisational consultants Stanton Marris. It has its roots in organisational psychology and hypothesised that there are four areas of experience that either energise or de-energise people in their work place. These have to do with:

1. Doing the kind of job you like doing
2. Being treated well by your line manager
3. Having the resources/support you need to do your job effectively
4. Believing in what the organisation stands for

Energy zones

Stanton Marris called them the '4 Cs: Content, Climate, Context and Connection'. I preferred to call them 'energy zones' - the focus being on what experiences energise or de-energise people in the workplace – and labelled them: 'Self-fulfilment', 'Line management', 'Supportive environment' and 'Engagement with the organisation'.

The validation took the form of presenting a list of forty-six statements to staff in a survey for a public sector organisation. The list included things like *'My manager makes me feel needed'*, *'I get the practical support I need to work effectively'*, *'I feel able to be myself in this organisation'* and *'I enjoy the tasks that my job involves'*. Staff were first asked to rate each one in terms of how often they felt each statement applied to their employer using a five-point scale ranging from *'Always'* to *'Never'*. They were then asked to rate each one according to how important it was in terms of energising them at work, irrespective of how far they felt it currently applied. The scale used was a five-point scale going from *'Essential'* to *'Not at all important'*.

The academics who had developed the original list of factors had also allocated each of them to one of the four categories. The question was, would these factors actually cluster together in this way when put to a sample of staff?

What the cluster analysis showed was that, largely, they did. Whether we took the dataset of responses to the first or the second question, the statements ascribed to each category were generally the ones that correlated best together. There were some that correlated reasonably well with statements from other categories, as well as their own. And this is just as you would expect; managers saying 'well done' reflects both in the experience of line management and in the supportive environment, for example.

A particular strength of this framework is that it feels intuitively right. We can all relate to it. If you think of the kinds of things that energise or de-energise you at work, you will probably find they all fall into one, or sometimes more, of these categories. Or think about other people we know or may have come across. A nurse working in a hospital who is passionate about caring for her patients (self-fulfilment) and is treated well by the senior nursing staff (line management), but is frustrated by lack of support staff (supportive environment) and the way some of the traditional values of the health service seem to be being eroded (engagement with the organisation). Or the IT boffin who enjoys the tasks being set (self-fulfilment) and the high standards and social responsibility of his employer (engagement with the organisation), but is disillusioned by the lack of investment in the latest software (supportive environment) and apparent unwillingness of his manager to listen to his concerns (line management).

I find it provides a powerful framework for running through the factors within the organisation that appear to be energising or de-energising staff.

However, it, like several other 'models', is essentially a framework for helping us to organise the research findings. It is one tool that can help us to understand better how different facets of the business are working and the issues we need to address. We still need to put these together with other things we know about the organisation in order to identify what should be done to address those issues.

Frameworks from academia

The second source of frameworks is from those who have made a study of organisations and have come up with their own frameworks of how organisations work. Rensis Likert would fall into this category since much of his research was about developing a theoretical understanding of how organisations work, underpinned by empirical research. The thing about such models is that they aim to embrace more than just employee attitudes and more than just what can be measured by employee surveys. Likert presented this model in his book 'New Patterns of Management'. [26]

Likert's schematic pattern of relationships showing measurements yielding prompt versus delayed information

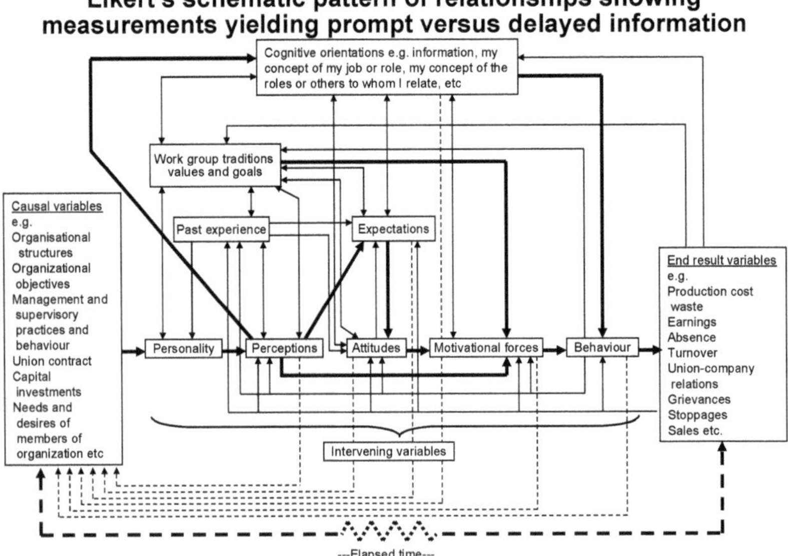

The following model was developed by WW Burke and GH Litwin27 in the 1970s and refined during the 1980s for British Airways to assist in its post-privatisation restructuring. It has also since been applied to various other organisations, including the BBC. A strong theme of the model is the idea that organisations have to respond and adapt to the external environment while getting all their internal systems and processes right and meeting the needs of individual employees.

The Burke Litwin Model

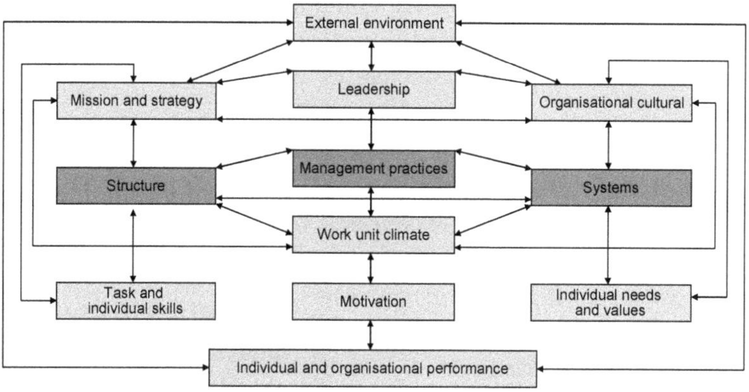

Frameworks from your own business models and plans

The third place to look to for frameworks is your own business models and plans. Hundreds of person-hours are usually spent on developing these plans that cover the overall business strategy or the strategies of particular areas or functions of the business. Particularly relevant for employee surveys are plans to do with HR and communications, but all should be reviewed.

These plans are critically important. They should represent the best and most up-to-date thinking on where the business is going and how it is going to get there. Moreover, they are unique to your particular organisation. No other organisation starts from where you start from or is heading where you are heading. Any process that sets about collecting information to assist the business should feed into these plans. If it does not, you have to wonder either what its use is or what the use of the plan is!

No other organisation starts from where you start from or is heading where you are heading

Employee surveys are no exception, yet it is amazing how many surveys are commissioned that consist of standard, off-the-shelf questions that are not customised at all to reflect the unique nature of the organisation or the plans that are supposed to lie at the heart of its development. It is too easy to be beguiled by the idea of measuring how well you are doing against international, or sector, norms and miss what should be the far more important purpose of the employee research: to see how well you are doing against the objectives of your business plans and to identify issues you should be addressing to realise these objectives more effectively.

Sometimes business plans will contain a clear model of how the business is perceived to work. Often this is implicit and it is worth spending time trying to make it more explicit so you can see how employees' feelings, attitudes, behaviours, knowledge and motivations work with your internal structures, processes, systems and core business thinking to realise its purpose.

It is too easy to be beguiled by the idea of measuring how well you are doing against international, or sector, norms and miss what should be the far more important purpose of the employee research

If your business has developed its own unique mission/purpose, corporate and brand values, aims, objectives, goals and business strategies, then your employee research needs to link into these. One starting point is to get it clear in your own mind how these things relate to the success of the organisation then how employee research can feed into them. Here is a framework I developed to help one organisation do just that:

Employee research and core organisational thinking

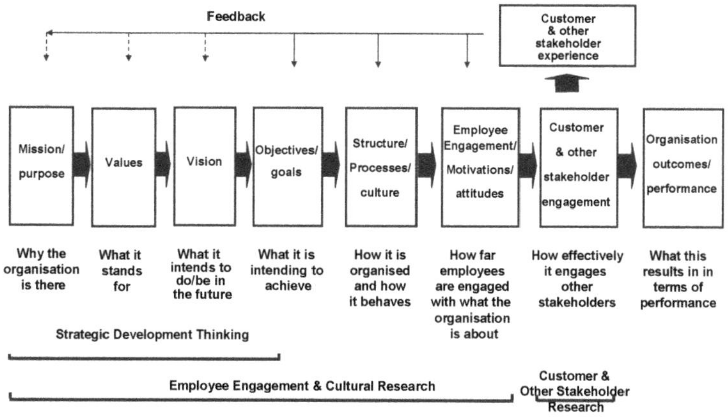

Feedback

Customer & other stakeholder experience

Mission/ purpose → Values → Vision → Objectives/ goals → Structure/ Processes/ culture → Employee Engagement/ Motivations/ attitudes → Customer & other stakeholder engagement → Organisation outcomes/ performance

Why the organisation is there | What it stands for | What it intends to do/be in the future | What it is intending to achieve | How it is organised and how it behaves | How far employees are engaged with what the organisation is about | How effectively it engages other stakeholders | What this results in in terms of performance

Strategic Development Thinking

Employee Engagement & Cultural Research

Customer & Other Stakeholder Research

It is very difficult for questionnaires that consist of standardised attitude statements using agree/disagree scales to engage with this kind of framework. They tend to come up with bland generic statements such as *'I am aware of (Employer's) values'* or *'This organisation is run on strong values/principles'* that really tell you nothing that you can do anything with. By drawing off a much wider range of question techniques, a good survey can understand how staff relate to the core thinking of *their own* employer and how well this is being realised throughout the organisation.

By drawing off a much wider range of question techniques, a good survey can understand how staff relate to the core thinking of their own employer

The long term trend has been towards companies being more explicit about why they exist – their purpose or mission – what they are trying to achieve - their vision – and what they stand for – their values. The 'think tank', Tomorrow's Company, outlined in its Tomorrow's Global Company report[28] how major companies have to adjust to the changing environment in which they operate, not least due to the massively changing expectations that all their stakeholders have of them. The report notes how tomorrow's global company needs to expand and redefine its view of success, embed values that are necessary to provide cohesion to diverse, global enterprises and work with governments and other parties to develop appropriate frameworks to underpin a sustainable future. Major companies are at various stages along the road to doing this, but what it flags up is that all companies have to change to survive. An important part of this survival is taking your staff with you. What this is likely to mean is being responsive to the expectations of your employees and involving them in the development and implementation of the company's success model, its values and even the frameworks in which it operates. Employee research can help but it needs to recognise, as Tomorrow's Company does, that every business is on a different path and needs to work out its own route map rather than simply adopt 'off-the-shelf' solutions.

Frameworks from your own experience, intuition and imagination

A well-constructed survey is likely to produce a great deal of information about your organisation that you did not know before. Moreover, of course, it is not the only kind of information that you have available to tell you how the business is working (yet to see some of the ways in which researchers have attempted to 'model' the data, you would think it was). The challenge is to develop some simple frameworks that allow you to understand better what is going on in your business and in a way that you can easily communicate to others. Thus, the third source of frameworks is your own experience, intuition and imagination!

The challenge is to develop some simple frameworks that allow you to understand better what is going on in your business

Developing such frameworks can be a very satisfying thing to do, especially to round off a presentation containing scores of charts and hundreds of figures. Try bringing it all together onto one page that is not just a lot of bullet points!

Here is a chart I developed for one organisation, a local authority, to bring together the results of its employee survey and relating it to the big issues of the organisation. What was coming through from both a range of different types of quantitative questions (none of which used an agree/disagree scale!) and complementary open-ended questions, was a whole series of interrelated issues, but most of them had to do with the number of staff they had, their training and skill levels and equipment and technology.

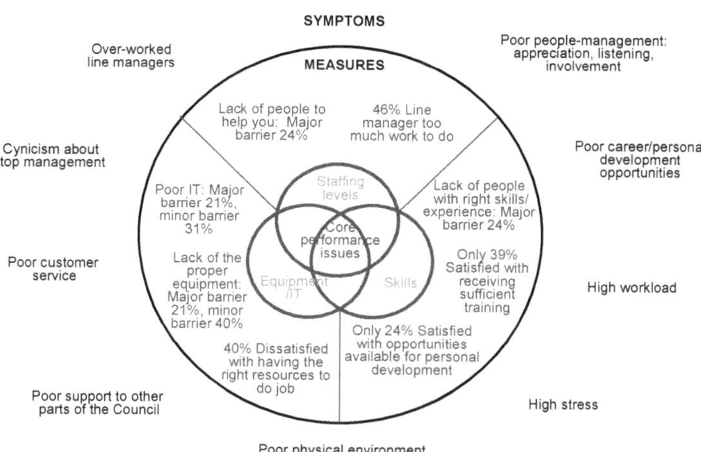

This particular chart was designed to focus on what we termed 'performance issues'. Indeed, the questionnaire divided into three broad categories of questions:

1. Those relating to the performance of the organisation - designed particularly to identify the things that were holding it back
2. Those relating to the employees and the factors driving their job satisfaction and motivation
3. Those reflecting different aspects of the corporate culture

What it demonstrated to the client was that staff had a very clear view on what was stopping them performing much more effectively and that many of the measures we were collecting were really symptoms, not causes, of the underling issues that management had to address. Had we gone the route of having a questionnaire that consisted solely of attitude statements against an agree/disagree scale, it would not have been possible to ask the kind of direct, penetrating questions needed to build up this kind of picture.

Organisations do not exist to serve themselves. Their ultimate purpose is to serve external stakeholders, not least their customers, but also suppliers, investors, regulators, local communities and so on. It is surprising how often this simple fact gets overlooked in constructing an employee survey. Questionnaires can focus on lots of different facets of the internal culture without any apparent acknowledgement of what the organisation's ultimate purpose is, whether it is to manufacture dog food, run a care home or deliver train services efficiently. When constructing an employee survey, it is worth reflecting on how you fulfil your ultimate purpose and create value for your various stakeholders.

When constructing an employee survey, it is worth reflecting on how you fulfil your ultimate purpose and create value for your various stakeholders

I developed this chart to illustrate just that point for the local authority mentioned above.

What drives customer satisfaction?

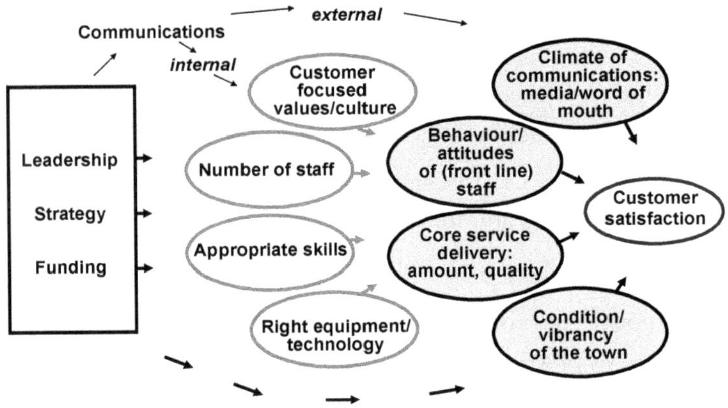

Working right to left, the model started with customers, recognising that, ultimately, the council is there to meet their needs and to improve/maintain their overall satisfaction. It then identifies four categories of factors that the local authority can influence that impact on customer satisfaction. It then defines four kinds of internal factors that determine, in particular, core service delivery and (front line) staff behaviours. Finally, it recognises that behind these lie the overall frameworks, structures and constraints (such as budget) of the organisation and the important role of both internal and external communications.

This framework helped management to appreciate the systemic nature of what they were dealing with. It is very easy to get obsessed with one aspect of the problem – leadership, communications, funding, resources and so on - and overlook the fact that all these things are interrelated and need to be tackled together if you are to achieve the ultimate desired outcome.

Bespoke frameworks developed with professional facilitators

If you were really committed to undertaking a root and branch review of the business, then the ultimate framework would be one developed uniquely for and by you, working with a professional facilitator. One of the best in the business is a company called Group Partners Limited. It specialises in making highly complex systems simple and accessible. Its unique approach, the brainchild of its founder, John Caswell, is called 'Structured Visual Thinking™'. This involves working closely with a company's senior management to develop a highly visual, systemic, multilayered, conceptual, diagrammatic, pictorial and verbal model of how their client's business works. The approach has enormous advantages over a generic approach. These include the fact that whatever it produces is unique to the organisation; its senior management can really relate to it since they were intimately involved in its development; it is highly systemic so that you can see easily how problems in one area can have knock-on consequences in other parts of the system. So long as they are designed with the framework in mind, employee surveys can be extremely useful at flushing out the various 'Contextual Frameworks™' that make up the whole system. Quantitative measures or verbatim comments can be used to illustrate what staff know, think, do and feel, and why, across different parts of the system. In turn, the contextual frameworks can help you understand how staff behaviours, attitudes, knowledge, motivations and feelings contribute to making the rest of the system work.

***Developing Structured Visual Thinking™**

*Reproduced with kind permission of Group Partners Limited

So which framework should you adopt?

The answer is probably a bit of each. Your framework should definitely relate to your overall business plan, otherwise, it is no use at all. Your own experience, intuition and imagination are critical to make sense of the uniqueness of your own organisation. The academic models/frameworks remind us that human organisations are complex systems that have many elements that interact together to achieve multiple purposes. If you are going to focus on one aspect e.g. employee attitudes, you have to recognise that they are just one piece of a complex and multidimensional jigsaw. However, academic frameworks are essentially generic. It is up to you to decide whether they can really be applied to your own organisation and, if so, how they should be adapted to enable you to link together everything you know about it to build a coherent picture that enables you to understand what you need to be doing to move the organisation forward. Having a professional facilitator assist you in developing your own frameworks can be enormously beneficial but you need to be in a position to follow it through.

Sadly, the least useful frameworks are likely to be the ones provided by employee research consultancies that are promoting a standardised set of agree/disagree statements. At best, they provide a reasonable list of areas that should be included in an overview employee survey. At worst, they proclaim direct links between their particular measures and organisational performance that do not really exist.

Sadly, the least useful frameworks are likely to be the ones provided by employee research consultancies

How the intangibles work

Most of the innovative business literature of the last 40 or so years might be seen as contributing to our understanding of the nature of value creation. Whereas most of the language of business and economics used to be about the nature of tangible assets and how they could be used to create economic value, now it is increasingly recognised that value is essentially intangible and the factors that drive and facilitate it are also intangible.

Now it is increasingly recognised that value is essentially intangible and the factors that drive and facilitate it are also intangible

The framework below illustrates what I mean. It was born out of a realisation that, although businesses include very clever people in their different functions - finance, marketing, HR and so on - the reality is that they are each trained to think of the business in different ways, and ways that, by and large, do not connect well together. Those in finance tend to think in terms of the tangible assets of the business, with cash flow as the ultimate objective. Those in marketing or HR have quite different perspectives.

In this model, people are a tangible asset, but what they know, do, think and how they interact with one another and with external stakeholders are all part of the intangible equity of the business.

How intangible equity drives value

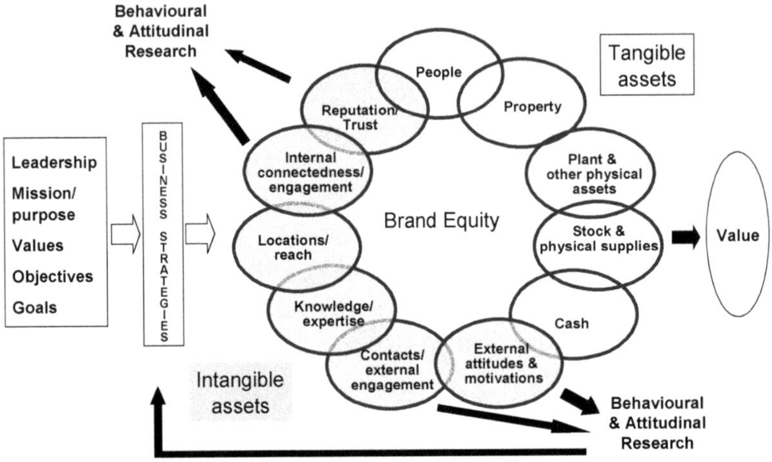

Behavioural & Attitudinal Research
Leadership
Mission/ purpose
Values
Objectives
Goals
BUSINESS STRATEGIES
People
Property
Tangible assets
Reputation/ Trust
Internal connectedness/ engagement
Plant & other physical assets
Brand Equity
Locations/ reach
Stock & physical supplies
Value
Knowledge/ expertise
Cash
Contacts/ external engagement
External attitudes & motivations
Intangible assets
Behavioural & Attitudinal Research

It was only when I had developed this model and started thinking about the nature of these assets that I realised that each of these assets can be thought of as either *drivers* (they make things happen), *facilitators* (they are necessary for things to happen) or *outcomes* (they are what results from things happening) of the value creation process.

However, the critical thing about the intangible assets is that not only are they, like the tangible assets, *facilitators,* but they are also often *drivers* and *outcomes* of the value creation process. In other words, while property and plant cannot make things happen, people can. While property and plant cannot create more property and plant, knowledge and expertise can create more knowledge and expertise. The intangible factors in the organisation can multiply and help to drive and facilitate more value creation until the limits of the tangible assets are reached.

What the assets of the business do in the value creation process

INTANGIBLES	Facilitators	Drivers	Outcomes
Employee/organisational knowledge/expertise	✓		✓
Contacts/external engagement	✓	✓	(✓)
Internal engagement/culture/motivations	✓	✓	(✓)
Services supplied	✓		✓
Knowledge/awareness/attitudes in the market	✓	✓	(✓)
Reputation/trust	✓	✓	✓
Locations/reach	✓		(✓)
TANGIBLES			
People	✓		
Cash	✓		✓
Property	✓		
Plant and other physical assets	✓		
Stock/other physical supplies	✓		
Goods manufactured			✓

The value of this way of looking at things is that it demonstrates that the human resources of a business are quite different in nature from the tangible assets, and as such need to be managed quite differently. One of the key roles of employee surveys should be to enable us to understand how those intangible aspects of the organisation, that have to do with people and the way they interact, work to create value.

One of the great challenges that has so far eluded consultants in this field is the ability to link employee measures and cultural factors to organisational and particularly commercial, performance. One reason for this is that the data generally do not exist to demonstrate that high ratings on employee survey measures correspond to better commercial performance. The timeframes and business units in which data are collected usually do not correspond, the number of data units is normally too small and there are too many other factors involved in determining business performance that are not included in the model for conclusive analysis to take place.

However, arguably it is pointless trying to demonstrate that there is a measurable relationship between, for example, 'employee engagement' and organisational performance. It should be taken as a given that creating the right internal culture and systems and high levels of employee engagement, will result in improved performance. The main problem for HR people, and those that undertake employee surveys, is not that they cannot generate the clinching empirical proof of their belief that 'it is all down to culture' but that they are using a completely different framework to think about the problem to the finance people. They think the finance people want measures that demonstrate that higher attitude scores on their surveys generate improved business outcomes. In fact, the finance people already know that better, more motivated and committed staff add more value to the bottom line. It is just that they, understandably, cannot see how the generic measures produced from many of the questions asked in employee surveys, relate to the very specific business issues that they have to manage day-to-day.

It should be taken as a given that creating the right internal culture and systems and high levels of employee engagement, will result in improved performance

I hope that this model helps to put the role of staff into perspective and within a common framework that all the different roles of the business can relate to.

PART 4

Summing up: the agree/disagree fallacy

PART 4: Summing up: the agree/disagree fallacy

This book started with a mystery: why was it that most leading employee research consultancies have defaulted to questionnaires that consist almost exclusively of agree/disagree scale questions. Having written the book, although I have developed certain ideas on why this might be the case, I am not sure I am much closer to the answer. Nevertheless, the journey has enabled me to clarify my thinking about the pros and cons of this approach.

I have no particular issue with agree/disagree scales, which I have been using for over 30 years. However, all techniques have their limitations. Because they do one thing, they necessarily do not do other things. My issue with the agree/disagree scale is with how this one technique has come to dominate the world of employee surveys and crowded out so many other question techniques that could do far more justice to the views of those employees who have taken the time to take part in an employee survey.

It seems to me that the belief that employee questionnaires should consist (almost) exclusively of agree/disagree scale questions is a **fundamental fallacy** that has become embedded in many consultancies that undertake employee surveys. From this, other fallacies have followed. These include that:

- Agree/disagree scales are necessarily a better way of measuring attitudes than other scales.
- They are an effective way of measuring non-attitudinal aspects of the internal culture, particularly employee behaviours, knowledge and motivations.
- There are significant advantages in having all your data in the same format so that multivariate analysis can be carried out and that these advantages outweigh the advantages of not doing so.

- Business performance is best enhanced by companies focusing on improving their ratings against normative measures derived from agree/disagree scales.
- The main, sometimes only, context for interpreting results should be how an organisation's scores compare with the consultant's normative measures.

I cannot but think that some of the ways in which the agree/disagree scale has been used and results interpreted by today's consultants would not have passed the high standards of research rigour that the founding fathers of organisational psychology, such as Rensis Likert, set for themselves. Although he is mainly remembered for his attitude scale, Likert makes it clear in his book, 'New Patterns of Management', that organisations need to be defined by far more than just the attitudes of their employees. He refers, for example, to 'causal variables such as the organisational structure, and the behaviour of managers and superiors'[29] which are outlined in his schematic diagram (reproduced on p138).

What I have tried to show in this book is that surveys are a very useful aid to management. Used correctly they can be performance enhancing for the organisation and liberating for employees. Used incorrectly they can at best tell management nothing they can use, at worst point them in entirely the wrong direction. I hope this book will help managers apply the right survey tools and point them in the right direction.

About the Author

Peter Hutton is founder and managing director of BrandEnergy Research. After graduating with a degree in Social and Political Sciences from Cambridge in 1974, he joined the London-based market and opinion research firm, MORI. He spent the next 29 years undertaking various kinds of research and learning about the practical arts of management. His first book, Survey Research for Managers, was published in 1988. He was made a director of MORI in 1988 and deputy managing director in 2000. In 2003, he left to set up BrandEnergy Research Limited following a management buy-out. He is a member of the Market Research Society, the Marketing Society, the International Association of Business Communicators, the Local Authorities Research and Intelligence Association, the Independent Consultants Group, Tomorrow's Company and The Lamberhurst Corporation.

His hobbies include three children, Scouting and managing a Little League football team.

Index

Index

References

1 Breaking down barriers: Reconstructing market research for the 21st Century, ESOMAR Congress 2006

2 See Best Companies Methodology on www.bestcompanies.co.uk

3 Pamela L. Alreck and Robert B. Settle, 'The Survey Research Handbook' Irwin McGraw Hill, 1995 p116

4 © BrandEnergy Research/IPSOS MORI

5 See Hutton, Peter, Employee Advocacy, published in the Managing Partners' Forum '100 Best Professional firms to work for 2008', April 2008, available from www.brandenergyresearch.com/papersandarticles.htm

6 See Best Companies Methodology on www.bestcompanies.co.uk

7 Buckingham, Marcus and Coffman, Curt, First Break All the Rules – What the World's Greatest Managers do Differently, Simon & Schuster, 1999

8 Ibid, p14

9 Ibid, p20

10 Ibid p20

11 Ibid, p281

12 Ibid, p20

13 Ibid, p20

14 Ibid, p282

15 Ibid, p285

16 Ibid, p20

17 Ibid, P26

18 Ibid p282

19 See Best Companies' website www.bestcompanies.co.uk

20 See Best Companies' Methodology on www.bestcompanies.co.uk

21 Best Companies Methodology p12

22 Ibid. p20

23 See the ISR Surveys Engagement Fact Sheet via its website

24 First Break All the Rules, pp295-6

25 "Play to Your Strengths", Mercer

26 Likert, Rensis, New Patterns of Management, McGraw-Hill, 1961. Reprinted by permission of McGraw-Hill.

27 Burke, W.W. and Litwin, G.H., A causal model of organizational performance and change. Journal of Management, Vol.18, No. 3, pp523-545 copyright © 1992. Reprinted by Permission of SAGE Publications.

28 Tomorrow's Company, Tomorrow's Global Company, Challenges and Choices, 2007

29 Likert, Rensis, New Patterns of Management, p197, McGraw Hill, 1961, p201.

www.ingramcontent.com/pod-product-compliance
Ingram Content Group UK Ltd.
Pitfield, Milton Keynes, MK11 3LW, UK
UKHW020251250726
13967UKWH00004B/1605